Addiction Recovery:
A Family's Journey

Revised Edition

By

Diana Clark, JD, MA

Family Healing Strategies

www.familyhealingstrategies.com

For information on Diana Clark's family healing workshops, lecture series, intervention services, individual family coaching services, and other services, please visit the website www.familyhealingstrategies.com.

Diana is also the author of the audio book "What Love Looks Like: When Your Adult Child Struggles with Addiction." You can order the audio book online at www.familyhealingstrategies.com.

To order multiple copies of this book, please contact Family Healing Strategies at familyhealingstrategies@gmail.com.

ISBN: 1492862339
ISBN-13: 978-1492862338

Dedication

For the dedicated and loving family members of those who struggle with addiction

And for Donn, Eli and Will

.......and for Katie Bird.

All of the case studies, events and anecdotes discussed in this book are true, although some of the case studies are an amalgam of multiple families. Names, places and identifying characteristics have been altered to preserve anonymity.

Acknowledgments

No book is written without significant contributions by others. In particular, this book would not have been completed without the support of my family as well as my friends and colleagues: Tammy, Ann, Randi, Charlie, Karin, Mary, Sarah, Arden, Bruce, Laura, Peter, Patrick, Woody, Bruce, John, Catie and Kevin. Also, I am indebted to Ann Overbeck, editor extraordinaire, for polishing the rough edges to reveal a book of which I am proud.

Contents

Continuous Trama

Impulse Poop — disintegration of
adult Functioning

Boredom — necessary Ph 3

Happy ≠ Euphoric

"Move a muscle to change a thought"

Co-dependence — family addicted to
control addict

Depressed vs Happy

June 3 — next

Introduction

The phone rings. I hear a sobbing voice on the other end of the line. I listen. Out pour stories about a child, spouse, sibling, or parent who is drinking alcohol excessively, smoking marihuana, and/or using cocaine, meth, amphetamines or heroin. I listen.

Sometimes, a multiple-year history of drug or alcohol use is condensed into five minutes. Other times, it takes hours for the story to emerge. The vulnerability with which I am asked "Is it my fault?" or "Is there any hope?" or "Is my son going to die?" is heart-wrenching.

When the distraught family member and I talk, I congratulate him for asking for help, and I offer:

"You are not alone."

"There are great treatment options."

"I have seen mind-blowing transformations from what you are now calling an 'addict scum' to a remarkable human being."

"What counts are the actions you take now."

And I emphasize, "Your love, when properly channeled, can help your loved one."

I have seen this kind of love. As a specialist in family addictions, I have witnessed extraordinary examples of love by ordinary people. Family members love when it is painful to love, when they are full of anger. A mother loves fiercely with tears running down her cheeks. A brother loves when he is terrified.

If you are reading this book, it is likely that you have an addicted or alcoholic child, spouse, sibling or parent and that you are desperately searching for answers. I imagine that you lie awake at night asking yourself over and over "How can I fix this?" or "How can I change this?" or, in the worst of times, "How can I make my child go away?" Your dreams shattered, you are afraid that your life and the lives of your family members will always be devastated by addiction.

Let me reassure you that I have witnessed people in your situation gather up their reserves of strength, change their actions to reflect an understanding of addiction, establish healthy boundaries, and become more compassionate and empathetic in the process. Likewise, I have witnessed formerly active addicts and alcoholics, now in long-term recovery, become startling examples of the best of humanity. Then I question:

What if addiction isn't a curse?

What if life in recovery isn't a diminished life?

What if addiction is the catalyst for an addict or alcoholic to live with depth, humility and meaning?

Addiction can be a launching pad. Healing brings addicts and alcoholics closer to living life with integrity and self-reflection and in service to others. This journey from addict or alcoholic to fully functional adult is called *recovery*. Simply defined, recovery is the practice of behavioral, psychological and spiritual changes, beginning with abstinence, that encourage (and reflect) a healthy life.

Your addicted loved one's progression from active addiction to recovery and his success in long-term recovery will almost always involve you. And, just as your loved one needs a path toward healing, you need a path for your journey, which will take you from denial, protecting, and codependent behavior, and the underlying fear, to surrender, forgiveness, self-care, purpose, and meaning, and, ultimately, to gratitude for the gifts of your journey. This kind of change does not happen overnight.

This book maps out a path for your journey. Although the journey may feel long and will be painful at points, you may well find joy and peace at the end of it. And, even during the journey, you might find a spark for starting to live with joy and peace.

This book is essentially the workbook that I use to conduct family healing workshops. The book includes factual information, psychological theory, case studies, exercises, and a bit of folk wisdom.

The case studies involve individuals and families with whom I have worked directly as a family addictions consultant. Although each family is unique and each situation is different, the case studies can provide insight into your behavior or the behavior of your addicted loved one. And, although many of the case studies are about adolescents and young adults, the stories of addiction are applicable regardless of age.

The exercises are designed to provoke the kind of thought that leads to understanding. There is no single right answer to any of the questions. This is your personal journey of change.

So let us begin.

PHASE I: What's Happening to My Loved One?

Your journey starts with learning about the disease of addiction and its contributing factors and payoffs and discovering that there is real hope for your addicted loved one in recovery, the time-tested path toward healing.

Chapter 1   The Disease of Addiction

Time and again, the family member who reaches out to me describes feelings of horror and consternation at the revolutionary changes in a once loveable and sensitive (or thoughtful or considerate) child, spouse, sibling, or parent. Before substance abuse changed her, I am told, she was shy, awkward socially, or a little out of sync with the rest of her peers, or, instead, a superstar, a high school class president or captain of industry and the leader in her social circle. Sometimes I hear she is creatively gifted; most of the time I hear about her inborn intelligence.

Sadly, the upshot is always that a once praiseworthy loved one has become an empty shell of the person she was. Instead of furthering a healthy and productive life, she is applying all of her charm, gifts and intellect in the service of getting, using, and funding her substance of choice.

Despite the devastating changes addiction brings about, however, many of the family members who seek my help find it difficult to believe that their loved ones have a *real* disease. You may have the same feeling about your addicted loved one. Basically, you wonder: *His behavior seems so voluntary; why doesn't he just stop using?*

Reliable scientific research confirms what your addicted loved one's behavior suggests: addiction is a disease and addiction, the disease, disrupts the brain and its functioning.

Addiction Is a Brain Disease

"Drug addiction is a brain disease. Although initial drug use might be voluntary, once addiction develops this control is markedly disrupted." These are the words[1] of Nora D. Volkow, MD, Director of the National Institute on Drug Abuse (NIDA), which is a scientific research institute under the National Institutes of Health in the U.S. Department of Health and Human Services.

Our human brains are thought to be one of the most amazing and complex organic systems in the universe. Each year, researchers provide us with startling new information about addiction and the brain. Based on brain scan images conducted with cutting-edge technology, most experts agree that addiction (or even substance abuse without addiction) alters the brain. The brain changes can be long-lasting and can lead to the exhibition of previously uncharacteristic behaviors on a regular basis, including lying, manipulating, and stealing.

Addiction Alters Several Regions of the Brain

The Brain Stem

The brain stem is the stem-like region at the base of the brain that is connected to the spinal cord. The brain stem controls basic life-sustaining functions, such as heart rate, breathing, and sleeping. Different substances affect this area in different ways. For example, when taken in excessive

---

[1] Posted on www.drugabuse.org (NIDA's consumer education website).

amounts, opioid drugs and alcohol can repress the functioning in the brain stem to the point where the user stops breathing.

The Midbrain

The midbrain, which is part of the brain stem, is responsible for several elements of human functioning, including ascertaining threats to survival and registering pleasure. An addicted brain may interpret pleasure to be linked singularly to his drug of choice and the absence of the drug as a threat to his survival. Many alcoholics have relayed, "I didn't want to drink. I needed to drink." That need may feel similar to the need we have for food, water or even air. One friend of mine said that when he was in the midst of a heroin craving it was as if someone had put a plastic bag over his head and he "couldn't quite get enough air."

The Prefrontal Cortex

Located behind the forehead, the prefrontal cortex is the judgment center of the brain. A functioning prefrontal cortex controls impulsiveness, decision-making, and even our human sense of personal morality.

Drugs and alcohol disrupt the prefrontal cortex, which leads your addicted loved one to lie, to steal, to manipulate, to bully, and to whine without remorse. He acts without a sense of future consequences or a moral compass.

Very instructive is the case of Phineas Gage, one of the most famous and influential cases in neuropsychiatry. As the story goes, in 1848, Phineas was 25 years old and the foreman of a railroad construction crew. The crew was excavating rock in preparation for laying track near Cavendish, Vermont.

Phineas was packing sand over an explosive charge set in the rock with a tamping iron that weighed 13+/- pounds and measured 43" in length and 1.25" in diameter at its wider end. When the charge detonated unexpectedly, the tamping iron shot upward, entering Phineas' head under his left cheek bone, exiting at the top front of his head, and flying a number of feet until it landed on the ground.

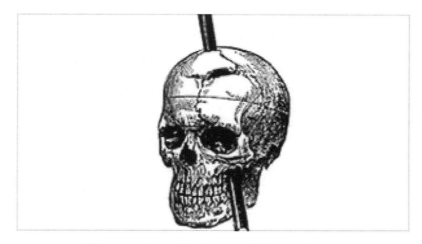

Illustration of Injury to Phineas Gage

Remarkably, Phineas survived. He was treated by a local doctor, John Martyn Harlow, MD, who is credited with performing one of the first-ever neurosurgeries, and Phineas returned home after only 10 weeks of care.

At first, although there was severe injury to Phineas' left prefrontal cortex (and probably his right prefrontal cortex), he appeared to have suffered no lasting effects of the accident other than a lost left eye. He walked, talked, ate, and engaged in all basic functions necessary for survival. As time passed, however, it became apparent that the accident had radically altered Phineas' character. Dr. Harlow documented the character changes in a case report in 1868, 20 years after the accident; the following is an excerpt from that report, which was printed in the *Journal of the Massachusetts Medical Society:*

> [Phineas' employers], who regarded him as the most efficient and capable foreman in their employ previous to his injury, considered the change in his mind so marked that they could not give him his place again. He is fitful, irreverent, indulging at times in the grossest profanity (which was not previously his custom), manifesting but little deference for his fellows, impatient of restraint or advice when it conflicts with his desires, at times pertinaciously obstinate, yet capricious and vacillating, devising many plans of future operation, which are no sooner arranged than they are abandoned in turn for others appearing more feasible. In this regard, his mind was radically changed, so decidedly that his friends and acquaintances said he was "no longer Gage."

Because drugs and alcohol affect the same area of the brain that Phineas injured, the reported changes in him probably mirror many of the character changes you have observed in your addicted loved one (absent the spike, of course). Unlike with Phineas, however, the damage to your loved one's brain did not occur instantaneously.

Drug Tolerance and the Power of Addictive Thoughts

Addiction happens in stages. When your addicted loved one initially got drunk or got high on cocaine or heroin or amphetamines, the experience produced such an intense euphoric pleasure and sense of well-being that her brain said, "Pay attention to this!" Yet, although her brain registered a profound experience, it was only temporarily altered by the drug. However, repeated doses, particularly if strung close together in a binge, would trigger changes in her brain.

Basically, to compensate for your addicted loved one's drug use, her brain produced fewer of its own feel-good chemicals, one of which is a neurotransmitter called dopamine. Therefore, after a binge, your loved one felt depressed and anxious. So she felt a craving to repeat the euphoric experience. Yet, because of the reduced level of dopamine, she needed a higher dose to achieve the same level of euphoria she had the first time she used; this is called drug tolerance.

In summary, regular drug-taking creates a greater and greater tolerance. As the tolerance develops, it morphs into dependence. At this point, your loved one not only needs the drug to get high but also feels bad in its absence.

Drug dependence, in turn, can lead to further changes in your addicted loved one's brain. Given his brain's reduced production of dopamine on its own and the escalation of his need, or craving, for the drug, your addicted loved one constantly thinks about the drug his body so desperately craves. Just as a person who is starving can only think about food—preparing it, eating it, smelling it, tasting it—your addicted loved one obsesses about alcohol or other drugs. *How can I use? Where do I score? Who can I con for the money? How can I get away with using?*

As these thoughts whirl through his brain, day in and day out, they have the power to change his brain. Specifically, based on the research of psychologist Dr. Donald Hebb, a pioneer in neuropsychology, mental activity (thoughts) can change the neuronal structure of the brain by creating a new set of neural pathways. Hebb's saying was, "When neurons fire together, they wire together," according to the book *Buddha's Brain: The Practical Neuroscience of Happiness, Love & Wisdom*, by Rick Hanson with Richard Mendius. The *Buddha Brain* authors add, "As a result, even fleeting thoughts and feelings can leave lasting marks on your brain, much like a spring shower can leave little trails on a hillside."

The "lasting marks" made by addictive thoughts make subsequent addictive thoughts easier and easier. Extending the hillside analogy, rainwater from subsequent showers streams down the hillside in the trails left by the spring shower, rather than elsewhere on the hillside.

The good news is that the corollary principle "use it or lose it" is also true. When your addicted loved one's patterns of thinking are diverted, the neural structure supporting addictive thoughts shrinks and a new one develops. Thus, addicts can, and do, change their neural structures for the better when they engage in the recovery process. In the hopeful words of Peter Lazar, LCSW, Senior Regional Director of Clinical Outreach for Elements Behavioral Health in CT and NY, "People get good at being addicts through repetitive behavior. The same is true for recovery."

[Begin exercise 1.1]

Exercise 1.1: Changes in the Brain

Check the boxes next to the behaviors that your addicted loved one exhibits.

Purpose: To examine the possibility of changes in the brain of your addicted love one as a result of addiction.

- ❑ Lies frequently
- ❑ Answers evasively
- ❑ Lacks accountability
- ❑ Uses poor judgment
- ❑ Engages in frequent blaming
- ❑ Manipulates others
- ❑ Uses emotional blackmail
- ❑ Keeps distant from family members
- ❑ Engages in disrespectful behavior
- ❑ No longer talks about meaningful subjects
- ❑ Expresses a change of goals
- ❑ Shows increased knowledge about substances and their effects
- ❑ Denies he has a drug problem
- ❑ Lacks age-appropriate coping skills
- ❑ Lacks planning skills
- ❑ Experiences memory loss
- ❑ Fails to follow through with promises or obligations
- ❑ Shows an inability to focus
- ❑ Displays a change in morality
- ❑ Increases risk-taking behaviors
- ❑ Acts emotionally volatile

[End exercise 1.1]

Addiction Is Progressive

Addiction, for those with the requisite genetic and environmental factors (discussed later), is a progressive disorder. Generally speaking, there are three stages in the progression from manageable use to lethal addiction: early-stage addiction, middle-stage addiction, and late-stage addiction. How quickly the disease evolves depends in part on the substance used. In the case of alcohol or marijuana, first use can progress to addiction over a period of months or years. Other substances, such as heroin, cocaine and meth, are quickly addictive, and the progression from first use to addiction often occurs within a few months.

Early-stage Addiction

In the early stage of addiction, your addicted loved one appears to be having fun. He is the first to come to the party and often the last to leave. He describes himself as "a partier," and all of his leisure activities revolve around the availability of alcohol or drugs. Most of his friends are similarly prone to abuse substances. Your addicted loved one has little or no concept of moderate drinking.[2] Because he appears to be having fun no one feels compelled to sound the alarm. Most families assume this is a passing phase and, for many, it is, especially if he is a young adult.

A sizable group of young adults abuse substances with a vengeance while in college or during their early twenties and simply "grow out of it" when the demands of adulthood interfere with being high. Others are

---

[2] The following are the alcohol consumption guidelines in the pamphlet "Worried about your drinking?" published by The Moderation Management Network, Inc.: for women, no more than 9 drinks per week and no more than 3 drinks per occasion; for men, no more than 14 drinks per week and no more than 4 drinks per occasion; and, for all, 3-4 non-drinking days per week.

revealed as addicts and alcoholics. With young adults, it is difficult to differentiate between partiers on the one hand and addicts and alcoholics on the other hand because a majority of the changes are internal and thus hidden. Therefore, your loved one may have, without your knowledge, crossed that invisible line from abuse to addiction, rendering his relationship with substances substantially more committed than it is for his non-addicted peers.

Middle-stage Addiction

When your addicted loved one progresses to middle-stage addiction, his behavior begins to cause you alarm. His consumption has increased, he is taking different types of drugs, and/or the consequences of his using are mounting. In middle-stage addiction, your loved one is more distant and isolated and probably slightly depressed. His interests have diminished, his motivation is erratic, his patience is minimal, and his anger surfaces with ease. You find yourself concerned, but rationalize to yourself and to other family members and friends that he still appears to be "functioning."

Late-stage Addiction

During late-stage addiction, there is little question that your addicted loved one has a problem. She is clearly on a path to destruction and almost anyone she comes in contact with is well aware of it. She has lost her job and injured her relationships with friends, siblings, children and/or other family members. Her remaining relationships are often limited to those who also have a close relationship with substances, *i.e.*, her "drinking buddies."

Contributing Factors to Addiction

Most addiction professionals concur that addiction develops with the intersection of two components: a hereditary or genetic predisposition and environmental triggers. (Genetic predisposition is discussed below, and contributing environmental factors are discussed in Chapter 2.)

Genetic Predisposition

"If you shake my family tree, beer cans fall down." ~Anonymous

It is unlikely that a single addiction gene exists; rather, scientists postulate that addiction stems from a combination of genes and an interaction among them. The dopamine and other "feel good" receptors (the pleasure center) in our brains appear to be genetically predisposed to finding some activities more pleasurable than others. For example, one person might be able to drink alcohol without any noticeable enhancement of her "feel good" neurochemicals, *i.e.*, her brain does not register alcohol as particularly pleasurable. She is less likely to think about drinking later, less likely to seek opportunities to drink, and less likely to become an alcoholic. Conversely, another person might describe her first encounter with alcohol or other substances as "the first time I felt comfortable in my own skin," indicating, at least in one significant manner, a predisposition to addiction. In short, people who experience euphoria when using a particular substance are more likely to repeat the experience and to create a neural pathway in the brain that leads to addiction.

Case Study: Jim

Jim grew up with his parents and nine brothers and sisters in an affluent area of a New England city. Jim describes his father as an alcoholic who consumed 70 to 80 drinks per week yet maintained a prosperous business and an active social life. The family had a keg on tap in the kitchen, and Jim's father filled up pitchers of beer and drank them like water.

By his late teenage years, Jim was an active drinker and, by his mid-twenties, he was an alcoholic. Not wishing to raise his children in the manner he was raised, Jim quit drinking and started in a Twelve Step recovery process when his wife was pregnant with their first child.

Jim modeled a sober life for his three children, two boys and a girl. However, despite Jim's solid recovery, his two sons became alcoholics and addicts.

Jim was flummoxed because he had assumed that his sobriety would provide the needed buffer from his family legacy. He researched the inheritability of addiction and found the following fact: boys with alcoholic fathers (whether actively drinking or not) are four times more likely to develop an addiction than boys without alcoholic fathers.

Chapter 2   The Benefits Gained and the Price Paid

"Addictions always originate in pain, whether felt openly or hidden in the unconscious. They are emotional anesthetics." ~Gabor Maté, MD, *In the Realm of Hungry Ghosts: Close Encounters with Addiction*

Numbing Pain and Avoiding Stress

Addiction may be viewed as your loved one's quest to change the way he feels. Indeed, for your loved one, because addiction has altered his brain, changing the way he feels has become synonymous with survival. So he continues to use despite the detriments. You observe this quest for substances, which seems to drive all of his daily activities, and wonder: *What feels so bad that he "needs" to be high?*

Physical Pain

Your loved one may have triggered his genetic predisposition to addiction when he first took prescription medication. For example, some addicts have reported that their experience with legitimately prescribed pain medication for wisdom-teeth extraction opened the door for addiction. And the drugs seemed to be the answer to all of their pain—physical, emotional, psychological, and/or psychiatric.

Emotional Pain and Stress

Many first-person accounts of addiction have a common underlying theme: using alleviates emotional pain or relieves stress. For example, an addiction professional may hear from an addict or alcoholic: "I was in pain being who I was and drugs answered that pain." or "I felt different from other people and alcohol and drugs reduced my anxiety and sense of isolation."

Psychological and Psychiatric Pain

Many addicts struggle with two conditions: addiction and a mental health disorder, whether diagnosed or undiagnosed. A person who suffers from both is said to have a co-occurring disorder. Attention deficit disorder (ADD), attention deficit hyperactivity disorder (ADHD), anxiety, depression, bipolar disorder and post-traumatic stress disorder(PTSD) are mental health conditions that often go hand in hand with addiction. In short, addiction can develop as a response to the pain your loved one feels because of his underlying mental disorder, *i.e.*, he uses alcohol or other drugs to numb the mental anguish associated with that disorder.

Co-occurring disorders need to be addressed during addiction treatment and throughout recovery. Bipolar disorder, for example, which is thought to be caused in part by a neural chemical dysregulation, generally responds well to appropriate medication. And, although the medication prescribed for bipolar disorder will not address addiction, even in its early stages, concurrent treatment of the bipolar disorder can make addiction recovery more successful.

Emotional Trauma

Traumatic events, such as major losses or physical or emotional abuse, not only produce pain they can change the brain. Some experts hypothesize that the changes in the brain resulting from a traumatic event make the sufferer more susceptible to addiction. Thus, if your addicted loved one

17

experienced a traumatic event, she may have begun to medicate her pain with drugs and alcohol soon after the event. The trauma then became so buried under the wreckage of her addiction that it went ignored.

[Begin exercise 2.1]

Exercise 2.1: Addiction as Medication
Check the boxes next to the issues or events that may have triggered your loved one's addiction.

Purpose: To assess contributing factors to your loved one's addiction.

   ❏ Physical pain

   ❏ Emotional pain

   ❏ Anxiety

   ❏ Extreme sense of boredom

   ❏ Lack of ability to connect with others, *i.e.,* isolation

   ❏ Psychological/psychiatric disorder of _____

   ❏ Physical or emotional abuse

   ❏ Divorce (his or a family member's)

   ❏ Death of close friend or family member

   ❏ Loss of a job

   ❏ Premature end to a career

   ❏ Unhappy move to a new town or school

   ❏ Failed school experience

   ❏ Dumped by a major love or close friend

   ❏ Lack of social circle

   ❏ Failure to "fit in"

   ❏ Unachieved scholastic expectations

   ❏ Unrealized career expectations

   ❏ Expectation of perfection

   ❏ Failed income expectations

   ❏ Debt or economic crisis

[End exercise 2.1]

Other "Benefits" of Using

Not only does using substances numb pain, using substances can also be an entry into a whole new social culture. In his book *Pathways from the Culture of Addiction to the Culture of Recovery: A Travel Guide for Addiction Professionals*, addictions expert William L. White discusses the sociological and cultural elements that support drug and alcohol use. He describes the personality adjustment that occurs during active addiction as often being promoted by a peer group. In many drug and alcoholic peer cultures, the very same behavior parents consider evidence of a deteriorating character is prized, such as an affinity for breaking the law coupled with street smarts.

[Begin exercise 2.2]

Exercise 2.2: Payoffs
Check the boxes next to the possible payoffs for your loved one's drug and/or alcohol use.

Purpose: To assess your loved one's hurdles to recovery.

- ❑ Experiences social ease
- ❑ Becomes part of a new group of friends
- ❑ Appears to have a stronger sense of belonging
- ❑ Feels less physical pain
- ❑ Gains courage; becomes a risk-taker
- ❑ Numbs emotional pain
- ❑ Reduces anxiety
- ❑ Feels more powerful
- ❑ Gets attention from concerned family members
- ❑ Possesses skills applauded by the drinking and/or drug culture
- ❑ Provides an outlet for risk-taking
- ❑ Enhances creative thinking
- ❑ Reduces inhibitions for performing
- ❑ Shows an increased ability to talk
- ❑ Provides an excuse for lack of functioning

[End exercise 2.2]

Recap: The Development of Addiction

1. An individual, often with a genetic predisposition for addiction, uses drugs and/or alcohol.
2. He finds pleasure in the experience.
3. He uses the substance to numb pain.
4. He discovers other benefits of using, *e.g.*, a new peer group.
5. He gravitates away from non-using friends.
6. His brain is changing each time he uses and with each thought he has about using.
7. It works for a while.

When the Solution Becomes the Problem

"No problem can be solved from the same level of consciousness that created it."
~Albert Einstein

Inevitably, your addicted loved one's solution to her problems becomes the problem. She has impaired or damaged the judgment center of her brain. Thus, her capacity to make sound decisions is compromised, and her life becomes messier and more chaotic. Yet, seemingly blind to the mounting problems, your addicted loved one continues to try to defend the *status quo* of her addiction. Like most addicts and alcoholics, she will not see the severity of her problems until she has sustained major losses.

If your addicted loved one is a young adult, the problem is compounded. Not only have her dreams and ambitions been derailed and not only is her insight into the costs of her addiction limited, she is emotionally immature. While her peers were wrestling with life decisions and confronting the dilemmas of adulthood, your addicted loved one numbed her feelings and

22

stalled as an emotional adolescent. Absent drugs and alcohol, she would have been forced to learn coping skills and behavioral lessons. Instead, she relied on drugs and alcohol to cope with life's struggles, and other life lessons languished.

Simply said, your addicted loved one has not matured at the same rate as her peers. And, as Chapter 3 explains, because of her emotional immaturity and lack of coping skills, a stint in treatment will not be the end-game solution for her.

[Begin exercise 2.3]

Exercise 2.3: Consequences

Check the boxes next to the consequences already experienced by your addicted loved one.

Purpose: To ascertain and to add up the consequences of your loved one's addiction.

- ❑ Legal problems
- ❑ Career problems
- ❑ Divorce
- ❑ Parental rights issues
- ❑ Financial problems
- ❑ Loss of friends
- ❑ Loss of dreams
- ❑ Family problems
- ❑ Health problems
- ❑ Physical trauma

[End exercise 2.3]

Chapter 3 Healing the Brain

There is no single cure for a broken brain, and there is no cure for addiction. There is just a path—recovery—which, for many, stops the disintegration of their lives and leads to a healing.

Recovery is more than simply living without an addictive substance. Recovery is the process of learning to live a full life, attending to mind, body, positive social interactions, and spiritual well-being. A panel of professionals convened by the Betty Ford Institute discussed "recovery" in the following terms:

> *Recovery* may be the best word to summarize all the positive benefits to physical, mental, and social health that can happen when alcohol- and other drug-dependent individuals get the help they need. Those who are in recovery are typically sober, working, and tax-paying parents and neighbors. These are the types of personal and social qualities that one might reasonably take pride in and publicly announce if one were seeking elected office or a position of responsibility within a corporation or community.[3]

There are a few possible introductions to a life in recovery. One first step could be a chemical dependency treatment program. Some addicts and alcoholics decide on their own to enter a treatment program, while others go to treatment under a court order or following an intervention. Alternatively, some addicts and alcoholics join Alcoholics Anonymous (AA) or another fellowship group as a first step toward a life in recovery.

---

[3] Special article, "What is recovery? A working definition from the Betty Ford Institute," The Betty Ford Institute Consensus Panel, Special Section: Defining and Measuring "Recovery," Journal of Substance Abuse Treatment 33 (2007), pp221–228.

Intervention

The Merriam-Webster Dictionary defines intervention as "the act or fact or a method of interfering with the outcome or course especially of a condition or process (as to prevent harm or improve functioning)." This definition exactly describes an addiction intervention.

Often facilitated by a professional, an addiction intervention is a structured group meeting among family members and their addicted loved one. An intervention is designed to pierce addictive denial and to offer help to the addicted loved one in the form of previously arranged treatment. During an intervention, the family members, ideally in a loving and productive manner, confront their addicted loved one with the family's concerns about his damaging behavior, often reading statements or letters they have written, and they encourage their addicted loved one to seek treatment.

According to interventionist Woody Giessmann, LADC-I, CADC, CIP, who is the founder and CEO of Right Turn, Inc. in Arlington, MA:

> A broken family may need a good coach to get them to a place where they can express their concerns with love, a place where they can find meaning in the statement: We are coming together to support you because we love and believe in you. Away from the hurt, anger, and fear, family members can be led back to a kind and gentle place.

An intervention begins the family healing process by addressing the shame that parents feel, says interventionist Randi Coleman, MA, CADC, CAP. Randi adds:

> I am often told, "She is such a good person," but I already know that; addiction is not a moral dilemma and having an addict or an alcoholic in your family should not be shameful. Unfortunately, many families are ashamed. I reassure them that

they did not create this problem, but that family members can be instrumental in the solution. If I can make it safe for future addicts and their families to seek treatment with less fear and less pain, then I will have done what I set out to do.

Professionally facilitated interventions are enormously powerful agents of change. Not only does a well-run intervention address the need for family members to make hard changes, it usually results in addicted loved ones' accepting help. In fact, the statistics surrounding professionally facilitated interventions are remarkable: people go to treatment directly from an intervention 85 to 90 percent of the time.

Treatment

Addiction treatment is a first step for an addict or alcoholic toward stabilization and abstinence. Treatment can take a number of forms, including the following:

- Outpatient treatment
- Intensive outpatient treatment
- Day hospitalization
- Residential treatment
- Extended care
- Step-down programs (half-way houses and sober living residences)
- Individual therapy
- Group therapy

Treatment programs vary in approach and duration but they all provide a period of time without drugs and alcohol. In addition, they usually offer at least some of the following services: group therapy, one-on-one psychotherapy, cognitive behavioral therapy, nutritional education, relapse prevention education, psychiatric care, meditation and massage, physical fitness facilities and coaching, and other sober stabilization techniques.

Goals of Treatment

Most treatment programs utilize a variety of therapeutic techniques to accomplish the goals discussed in the following:

Pierce Addictive Denial

Long after your addicted loved one admits that addiction has made a chaotic mess of her life, she will most likely retain the illusion that she can drink alcohol or use drugs in the future. Treatment seeks to pierce this illusion through a variety of techniques.

Identify Relapse Triggers

Triggers are situations and objects that prompt thoughts about drugs. Addicts and alcoholics in recovery can be triggered to use drugs by seemingly innocuous events and associations. A professional can assess your addicted loved one's personal roadblocks and develop a plan to address each of his triggers.

Identify Motivations for Recovery

Almost everyone in a treatment program acknowledges that they are not living the life they thought they would live. Treatment can unearth your addicted loved one's motivations for changing his life so that he may begin to rebuild a healthy life.

Begin Addressing Underlying Pain

As discussed earlier, pain may be an underlying motivator for your addicted loved one's substance use. Although emotional trauma and significant pain may need long-term therapeutic services, most treatment programs seek to provide a safe place for your addicted loved one to begin addressing the pain of old issues.

Introduce and Encourage Healthy Coping Strategies

As is true for many addicts and alcoholics, your addicted loved one may have begun using drugs and alcohol in her teens. By relying almost exclusively on substances to cope with pain and discomfort, she now lacks other skills necessary for adult functioning. Treatment programs generally offer an introduction to healthy coping.

Introduce the Concept of Life in Recovery

As stated earlier, treatment is not recovery, just an introduction to recovery. Treatment programs provide the jumpstart for your addicted loved one to embark on a life-long journey of recovery. Peter Lazar offered the following insights about addiction treatment and its connection to recovery:

> People often call in crisis and are hoping deep in their hearts that once their loved one goes through treatment that their loved one will be "fixed." Those of us who work in the field know that this is just not possible. Recovery is a long process, filled with the highs and lows of living in the real world while trying to maintain some semblance of equilibrium. The fact is that people go into treatment scared, vulnerable, freaked out, and angry. The purpose of residential treatment is to provide a safe, loving, and professional environment to start the healing process. We do not fix. Our job is to provide medical and

psychiatric services to get people as physically and emotionally stable as possible. We will also provide tools for recovery in the real world.

How Long Does Treatment Take?

According to Nora Volkow, Director of the National Institute on Drug Abuse (NIDA):

> Individuals progress through drug addiction treatment at various rates, so there is no pre-determined length of treatment. However, research has shown unequivocally that good outcomes are contingent on adequate treatment length. Generally, for residential or outpatient treatment, participation for less than 90 days is of limited effectiveness, and treatment lasting significantly longer is recommended for maintaining positive outcomes.[4]

Determining the type of treatment and length of stay is an individual matter and best accomplished with the advice of one or more professionals, such as therapists, outreach professionals, interventionists and consultants. As tellingly stated by Robert S. Waggener, an experienced clinician and CEO of Foundations Recovery Network:

> If someone is highly motivated for change, they've truly hit "rock bottom" and have finally raised the white flag and surrendered, they'll get help at the Salvation Army, sleep on a cot, and eat beans at every meal if they have to. Most addicts are not in this stage of readiness and require far more sophisticated approaches to moving toward lasting change.

Will My Loved One Ever Be the Same Again?

After months or years of drug and/or alcohol use and then treatment, your loved one is different. You wonder: *Will this stranger disappear and the*

---

[4] Posted on www.drugabuse.org.

person I used to know return? The truth is that he will never be the way he was. If he doesn't stop using substances, his life will continue to deteriorate. If he embraces recovery, he will continue to change, although in many positive ways.

For most addicts and alcoholics, the brain damage sustained during years of addiction heals when three conditions are met: time, abstinence, and a program of recovery.

Time, Time, and More Time

Because it is likely that your loved one will still lack good judgment and healthy coping skills even after treatment, her treatment team may recommend additional services for her. Research shows that recovery rates significantly increase for those who are supported, monitored, and held accountable for remaining sober for a period of one year. As Arden O'Connor, MBA, CEO of O'Connor Professional Group in Boston, MA, explains:

> Addiction is a long-term, chronic disease, and its impact extends to families, friends and society at large. Inpatient treatment often starts the process of recovery, but it is not the solution to the problem. Research shows that maintaining sobriety one year post-treatment leads to better long-term abstinence rates, and some of the best outcomes for addiction stem from long-term monitoring, a practice implemented by the licensing boards for pilots and physicians.

In recent years, the relevant research has led to the development of excellent extended care programs and case management services designed to meet the long-term needs of addicts and alcoholics in recovery.

Abstinence

There is widespread agreement among addiction professionals that an addict or alcoholic in recovery must refrain from using *all* euphoria-creating substances, even substances he did not previously use. The rationale for total abstinence is:

1. The brain does not heal as well while exposed to euphoria-creating substances;

2. Addiction is a chronic disorder and, even when dormant or in remission, it will awaken when exposed to euphoria-creating substances; and

3. The brain will substitute one addiction for another, which is referred to as cross-addiction.

Time after time, parents tell me stories of cross-addiction. For example, I heard from one mother: "My daughter went to treatment for heroin addiction and now two years later she is a raging alcoholic."

Program of Recovery

A program of recovery provides the scaffolding for the healing brain. With the guidance and even tutelage of those already sober, your healing loved one can develop new, healthy neural pathways in his brain, develop new coping strategies for living a functional life, and address any character flaws that helped to open the door to his addiction.

Life in Recovery

Once your loved one has participated in a treatment program, the real work of recovery begins. Old coping mechanisms are off-limits, and your loved one still has to accomplish the following:

- Manage a life-long disease.
- Live sober.
- Change habits and behavioral patterns associated with drinking and using.
- Change the thinking that leads to thoughts of drinking and using.
- Change friends if her peer group was a factor in her substance use.
- Change goals if her prior goals are not conducive to recovery.
- Cope with the stress of everyday life.
- Develop new coping mechanisms for struggles and difficulties.
- *Change just about everything.*

That is a tall order, even for a fully functioning adult, and statistics have shown over and over again that support is essential to long-term recovery and a full life. As succinctly stated by Peter Lazar:

> You can't expect people to instinctively know how to live a healthy life if they haven't done so in years, even if they've been to rehab. Because we have taken away their "maladaptive crutch," and they have untested tools for life, a newly recovering person is just as vulnerable coming out of treatment as they are going in.

[Begin exercise 3.1]

Exercise 3.1: Adult Functioning Assessment

Check the boxes next to the statements that apply to your loved one most of the time.

Purpose: To assess how far your loved one has to go to achieve the maturity level of an adult.

- ❑ My loved one has good self-esteem.
- ❑ My loved one has the capacity to gather the resources to solve her problems.
- ❑ My loved one accepts advice.
- ❑ My loved one seems to understand that all behavior has consequences.
- ❑ My loved one is equipped to handle disappointment and pain.
- ❑ My loved one makes sound independent decisions.
- ❑ My loved one is emotionally mature.
- ❑ My loved one can ask for help.
- ❑ My loved one will accept no for an answer without manipulating to get what he wants.
- ❑ My loved one has good planning skills.
- ❑ My loved one follows through on promises.
- ❑ My loved one speaks respectfully when he disagrees with another person.
- ❑ My loved one takes responsibility for her finances.
- ❑ My loved one tells the truth.
- ❑ My loved one has an even temper.
- ☑ My loved one has the ability to empathize with others.
- ❑ My loved one has a healthy conscience.
- ❑ My loved one is physically responsible (takes care of her body).

❑ My loved one is assuming responsibility for his life (*e.g.*, is employed or is seeking employment).

❑ My loved one is assuming responsibility for his recovery (*e.g.*, goes to meetings, works with a sponsor, and/or receives other recovery-related therapeutic services).

❑ My loved one assumes responsibility for his mistakes (doesn't blame others).

❑ My loved one is genuine (doesn't wear a mask to please or to manipulate).

❑ My loved one has general optimism (instead of seeing herself as the victim).

❑ My loved one trusts others in a healthy way—not too much or too little; he has balanced, honest relationships.

❑ My loved one is sexually responsible.

❑ My loved one has realistic ambitions.

❑ My loved one has the capacity for self-control.

❑ My loved one is able to build successful relationships.

❑ My loved one is not abusive.

❑ My loved one has the ability to formulate and to carry out realistic plans.

❑ My loved one has the capacity for self-reflection and insight.

[End exercise 3.1]

Fellowship and Other Support Groups

Fellowship groups are particularly effective means of support and adjuncts to treatment. Notable examples are the national groups, such as Alcoholics Anonymous (AA), Narcotics Anonymous (NA), Save Our Sanity (SOS), and Smart Recovery, and more specialized local groups, such as groups that adhere to principles of Zen Buddhism. Fellowship groups are *not* treatment, but instead offer the ongoing support necessary for your loved one in recovery to initiate and to sustain changes in her life and in her thinking.

The most well-known fellowships, Alcoholics Anonymous (AA) and its offshoots, encourage change by endorsing a set of principles embodied in the Twelve Steps. These Twelve Steps and the related support materials address the behavior that led to, or justified continuing, drug and alcohol use. Participants in AA and other fellowships, by helping each other understand and abide by the Twelve Step principles and by addressing life's difficulties honestly and responsibly, have an invaluable, lifelong recovery resource.

One young woman in recovery described how support groups facilitated her recovery: "The person I was is still an addict. I had to become somebody else who wouldn't use drugs and I needed help to do that."

As a professional in the field and a sober man since 1995, Patrick B. provides his view on the role and importance of fellowship groups:

> Before any "miracle" can happen, certain steps must be taken to ensure the safety and success of the journey. First and foremost, I believe that those steps are the Twelve Steps of Alcoholics Anonymous. Beyond following the Twelve Steps of AA, it is imperative for an individual to seek out and accept a support group made up of men and women who have shared the same experience, strength, and hope, and who through their collective strength guide each other as peers along the path of recovery. Such a peer group will help the newly recovering

individual by showing them exactly how they were able to attain a continued stretch of sober time. Common traits in the lives of these men and women, just to name a few, are structure, responsibility, accountability, honesty, support, trust, and respect. Recovery takes time.

PHASE II: What's Happening to My Family?

This phase of your journey involves coming to terms with your loved one's addiction and the fundamental changes that will be required of you.

Chapter 4   Family Adjustment

Given that the actual changes to your addicted loved one's brain are invisible, you observe in panic as the person you love appears to be replaced by a person you no longer know. One devastated mother said, "If you asked me a year ago if my daughter would steal and then sell my engagement ring, I would have said absolutely not . . . but she did, and I have a pawn receipt to prove it."

One father said with tears in his eyes: "Her brain must not have been working. She traded her body for drugs."

One husband exclaimed with fury, "My wife drove a car drunk with our children in the car."

Motivated by your desire to prevent permanent damage, you prop up your addicted loved one by taking care of him and by assuming responsibility for problems that rightly belong to him. You tell yourself: "This is just a phase." or "Everyone drinks so much these days." or "She is so overworked." In short, you engage in denial and adjust your expectations and standards to maintain the illusion that your loved one is okay and your family is safe.

Driven by your fear, you become addicted to controlling your loved one. As a result, you get sick along with your addicted loved one, and your life diminishes as a result.

[Begin exercise 4.1]

Exercise 4.1: Evidence of Adjustment

Check the boxes next to the changes you have made to allow for your addicted loved one's behavior.

Purpose: To assess the ways your loved one's addiction has changed you.

- ☑ I have modified my view of what is normal.
- ☐ I no longer expect to be treated with respect.
- ☑ I do more and my addicted love one does less.
- ☑ I have adjusted my view of what is acceptable.
- ☑ I tolerate dishonesty.
- ☑ I tolerate small acts of theft.
- ☑ I make excuses for my addicted loved one.
- ☐ I used to dream that she would _____.

   Now I dream _____.
- ☑ I used to dream of the future; now I want to make it through the day.
- ☑ I no longer expect that my feelings will matter.
- ☑ I am happy if a conversation doesn't turn into an argument, even if nothing changes.
- ☑ I allow myself to be manipulated just to keep the peace.
- ☑ I let myself be badgered and bullied.
- ☐ I try not to think about my addicted loved one but find myself critical of everyone else.
- ☐ I have become controlling about things that don't really matter.
- ☐ I worry all the time but do not change what I do.
- ☐ I feel distant from the rest of my family.
- ☑ I blame my addicted loved one's drug and alcohol use on others.
- ☐ Other family members seem angry with me all the time.

[End exercise 4.1]

Denial in Action

Just as your loved one refutes that he is addicted, you and other family members have blind spots in your perceptions as well. Known as denial, these blind spots and other defenses abet you in sidestepping, minimizing, and explaining away events as something you imagined. Denial allows you to reject absolutely what is happening right in front of you.

Stories of denial range from complete obliviousness to a loved one's substance use to an awareness of the use unaccompanied by the willingness or capacity to address the issue appropriately. I have heard the following accounts:

- "My husband replaced all the clear alcohol with water. When I asked him about it he looked at me like I was nuts . . . and I believed him."
- "Carrie would disappear for days on end and then tell me it was my fault. I always seemed to be doing something wrong . . . and I would try to change."
- "Tommy had three DUIs in five months, and he convinced us that the cops in our town were after him."
- "I thought she was just smoking pot, even though I kept finding tiny glassine envelopes all over her room."
- "Every night while doing dishes I would complain about the disappearing spoons and my son would just look at me like I was a lunatic. I just couldn't figure it out."
- "The police in our small town seemed to be driving by our house a lot. . . . I thought a neighbor was in trouble."

- "We gave Leslie plenty of money every month to support her needs while living in a dorm, but she always needed more. Her computer broke, her cell phone disappeared, and she wanted to buy additional textbooks. . . . I thought she should just switch dorms."

- "George had the same friends from elementary school through eleventh grade. Then a whole set of new faces began to come to the house. I didn't know their parents; I didn't know anything about them except they looked different. They didn't make eye contact and barely acknowledged my existence. I thought they just had bad manners. It was the mother of one of George's old friends who finally told me what her son had been saying about George. Thank God she did. . . . I might still be in the dark had she not come forward."

- "My wife seemed to be doing laundry constantly. It was only later that I realized that was where she kept her liquor."

Although denial may lead you to make decisions you later regret, it is not a character flaw. It is a psychological mechanism your psyche employs when the truth is just too impossible to bear. In time, usually because things get worse, your denial passes.

Case Study: Penny

Penny worked in the hospitality industry in a resort area and was married to man from a well-to-do family. She relayed the following to me about her daughter Elizabeth.

"I knew Elizabeth was struggling. I knew she was drinking too much, getting into trouble—she was kicked out of a college dorm in New York City for drinking—but I was in total denial about how sick she really was."

"Lizzy is my gentle-spirited girl, who used to save insects and dream about fairies and princesses. She is the one of my three who didn't cause me trouble. Until recently, she was sweet, maybe a little anxious and forgetful, but still my same Lizzy."

"Charles (my oldest son) tried to tell me Lizzy was in trouble, but I ignored him. One night he came home and told me that he had just seen Lizzy get out of demolished Jeep, stumbling. I began to listen. As it turns out, I had missed a lot over the years. When the truth of how bad things were came to light, it came hard. My husband and I convinced Lizzy to go to rehab, and she agreed to go when a bed became available, which was in two weeks."

"Those two weeks were the longest of my life. Terrified that I had been in denial too long, I lay awake at night recalling every detail of her life, over and over. I was trying to figure out how we got to this place. I watched her like a hawk those two weeks, and it was awful. The mask that she had put on to keep the truth away from me came off and it was neither pretty nor sweet. She was irritable, nasty, and evasive. She wanted to go use, and I was in between her and her drugs. She snuck out of the house, and disappeared for hours at a time. I was a wreck; I lost 10 pounds in two weeks."

"The night before we were supposed to leave for rehab, Lizzy went missing again. I panicked, called all of her friends, and finally got the address of a crack house where she could be found. I got in my car and drove without even thinking about the potential danger of showing up at a crack house."

"A big, ugly guy covered in black tattoos answered the door, blocked my entrance, and told me to ######. I pleaded with him. I begged. I even asked him if he had a mother. Crying, I told him I was scared that my daughter was going to die in there. Something I said reached him. He threw Lizzy out of the house, and I stuffed her in the car. The whole ride home she berated me for interfering. The next day we got on the plane.

"A couple of weeks into her stay in rehab, Lizzy and her counselor called. 'Mom,' she said, 'I have to tell you that I have been using drugs intravenously.'"

"I was knocked to the ground. My daughter was an IV junkie? I just couldn't believe it. We live in a fabulous resort town, have money and privilege. . . . How could she be a junkie? Then I remembered the plastic tubing I found in her room a year or so ago while I was cleaning. I had thrown it away without a second thought. Since then I have tried very hard to keep my eyes open."

Family-wide Denial

Some family cultures support family-wide denial. The following describes two of the most common governing "rules" of those families: the "don't talk or ask rule" and the "don't tell anyone" rule. These rules are usually unspoken, but family members know they exist.

"Don't Talk or Ask Rule"

The "don't talk or ask rule" prohibits family members from talking about the problem at hand. Instead, they talk about the weather, Aunt Susie, or the food—anything but what they see, hear and feel.

Often, if one family member violates the rule, there are emotional ramifications. The addicted loved one and other family members get angry, sullen, distant, or defensive simply because the one family member tried to engage in honest communication about the problem.

"Don't Tell Anyone"

The "don't tell anyone rule" prohibits family members from telling the truth about a loved one's behavior to anyone outside the family. Not only does this ban on communication deprive family members of much needed support during times of addictive chaos, it leaves them vulnerable to the addicted loved one's manipulations. Sometimes it is only through the eyes of outsiders that family members begin to realize there is a problem.

[Begin exercise 4.2]

Exercise 4.2: Minimizing, Rationalizing, and Discounting

Complete the sentences below.

Purpose: To acknowledge the ways you have hidden from the truth.

I have denied my addicted loved one's substance abuse by telling myself the following:

_____

_____

I have minimized or discounted the seriousness of the situation by telling myself the following:

_____

_____

I have rationalized my addicted loved one's behavior in the following ways:

_____

_____

[End exercise 4.2]

Piercing Your Denial

Some describe their arrival at the truth about the seriousness of a loved one's addiction as a rapid rush of clarity, others as a slow dawning of reality. The overwhelming feeling that surfaces along with the truth is *fear.* Often, the fear is free-floating, nonspecific and striking without identifiable cause. Sometimes, the fear is specific and germane to the addicted loved one's actions, such as a fear that he will:

- Die.
- Become estranged from the family.
- Harm or kill someone else.
- Ruin his credit.
- Lose all that he has built.
- Continue to deteriorate.
- Never have a "normal" life.
- Never marry.
- End up in prison.

Even after you admit to yourself that your loved one is sick, your denial may still come into play. Because denial is, at its core, self-deception, willful ignorance about the disease of addiction and deeply held misconceptions about addiction remain fuel for misinformed action. You might talk and talk about the problem, might spend hours researching treatment options, and/or might consult an interventionist or counselor, but if you then ignore what you have learned, you will leave yourself and your entire family at the mercy of your addicted loved one.

Case Study: Randy

Randy, a sweet and gentle single father of his only child Adam, called me late one night, agitated and in a panic. He explained that Adam had recently been arrested for his third DUI and possession of heroin and needles. Randy was reasonably worried that Adam might be facing jail time, and Randy thought that a stint in treatment by Adam would be viewed favorably by the legal system.

According to Randy, Adam had recently dropped out of college, was living at home, and was smoking marijuana all day, every day, because he was convinced that marijuana was an effective medication for his anxiety. Notably, however, Adam's most recent arrest did not involve possession of marijuana, but rather possession of heroin and needles.

When I asked Randy about the source of funding for Adam's drug habit, Randy and I had a revealing conversation:

"How does he pay for his heroin?" I inquired.

Alarmed, Randy replied, "Adam doesn't do heroin. He was just holding it for a friend. He only smokes weed."

"Okay, how does he pay for his weed?" I asked, somewhat skeptically.

Randy replied, "I give him an allowance."

"How much?"

Pausing for a few seconds, Randy answered, "I used to give him $500 a week, but I have recently increased the amount."

I, very quietly and seriously, asked, "So how much money are you giving him every week for spending?"

"I guess around $100 to $150 per day, on average," Randy admitted.

"Randy," I said, as gently as possible. "Marijuana just doesn't cost that much. My professional advice is to get him admitted into a residential treatment center. I'm guessing he is a heroin addict. Have you talked with him about your concerns?"

"Oh, he would never sit still for that kind of conversation. He isn't ever willing to sit down and talk."

"I guess he has every right to refuse to talk with you but, Randy, you have every right to stop the flow of money. What you are doing now is likely financing a heroin habit and, unless you are comfortable continuing on that course, something has to change."

"Where would you recommend for treatment?" asked Randy.

I made some treatment suggestions, adding, "This may be a long haul, and you'll want to reserve some funds for aftercare and sober housing."

But Randy would not hear of it. He insisted, "Oh, you just don't know Adam. If he is willing to go, he will make it work. I told you he is a special kind of kid."

I tried to explain that we needed to go beyond the fact that Adam was special and to treat addiction for what it is, a disease, but Randy was no longer listening.

Bright and early the next day, I arrived at their house to meet with Adam and Randy. Despite having scheduled the appointment, Randy did not want to wake Adam, explaining, "He is so crabby when he first wakes up."

After three hours of talking in circles with Randy, I pushed the issue. "Just go and wake him, Randy," I urged. Randy disappeared.

The next thing I heard was a bellowing voice, *"Get ###### out of my room. How many times do I have to tell you this room is off limits to you?!"*

Randy returned to the living room, shaking his head, "I told you he was crabby. Now he won't talk to us."

"Did you tell him no talk, no more money?" I asked.

"No. He slammed the door before I got the chance."

"Come on, Randy" I urged. "Let's just go and talk to him through the door."

Eventually, after a lot of wheedling and cajoling, Adam opened his door, dressed in his boxers, stood in the doorway, and roared, "Who ###### are you?"

I explained to Adam that his father was worried about his legal problems and possible addiction and that I was there to discuss treatment options. Adam was furious.

"Tell [her] to leave," he said to Randy.

"No," Randy yelled. "You need help, and I've picked out the best and most expensive place for you to go."

After what seemed like hours of talking in the hall, Adam gave in and agreed to go to treatment. He appeared to be in the early stages of heroin withdrawal, and his father just wasn't going to yield. Arguing with each other every step of the way, they packed Adam's things and drove off.

Adam stayed in the facility for a five-day detox for heroin withdrawal. Then, Adam left the facility against the strong advice of the treatment physicians that he stay for treatment for a minimum of 28 days.

"Adam already knows what they would teach him there," Randy told me. I tried to argue the point, but for the first time since I had met Randy, he asserted a formidable boundary. "Adam is an adult. He needs to decide what is right for him, and I don't think treatment will make him happy."

I surrendered and wondered: *How can Randy just agree to let Adam come home as if nothing ever happened?* From deep within, I heard "Blissful ignorance, that's how." For despite all of the professionals' best efforts to educate Randy that detox is not treatment and even though Adam's chances of relapsing were astronomically high, Randy remained blissfully ignorant.

Denial is a powerful protective device. If you are like most people, you will need the advice and support of others to open your eyes to the things you just cannot or will not see. Although it may be difficult for you to dismantle generational family bans on involving outsiders, I urge you to take small steps. Only after you grasp the facts can you begin to gain insight into your reflexive responses and to make changes.

Chapter 5   Protecting Addiction

While your loved one is an active addict or alcoholic, you see things you wish you never saw, learn private information about your loved one you wish you never knew, and, if that is not hard enough, you must then figure out what to do with the information. As is usually the case, you naturally feel compelled to protect your addicted loved one from harm. You bail her out of jail, threaten her drug dealers, monitor her liquor supply, and call her friends. Instead of helping, however, your well-intended actions may fall into the category of behavior that is often called "enabling" or "protecting."

When you do things that ease the natural consequences of your addicted loved one's behavior, you are protecting the unhealthy and addictive behavior. Moreover, when you "over-function" for your addicted loved one by taking on the jobs she should do, you protect her addiction instead of promoting her growth. The more you and other family members take on, the less your addicted loved one feels the results of her behavior, and you and the other family members become weighed down with the additional responsibilities. The unintended effect is that you create rich opportunities for addiction to flourish without negative consequences, and you become sick and exhausted in the process.

"Enabling" or "protecting" then describes caretaking behavior that seeks to avert negative consequences for your addicted loved one. As well-intentioned as your actions might be, they have the effect of preventing him from experiencing the very things that are most likely to motivate him to seek help and to change: discomfort, struggle, and/or pain.

Protector status is not limited to family members. In fact, anyone in your addicted loved one's life can qualify as a protector: spouse, significant other, child, friend, clergy, employer, physician, law enforcement official, judge, or counselor.

"Protectors" believe that their actions, which are designed to ease pain, are helpful. But the opposite is true. Instead of promoting healthy change, the net result of "protecting" behavior is protecting addiction from treatment.

[Begin exercise 5.1]

Exercise 5.1: Are You Protecting Addiction?

Check the boxes next to behaviors in which you have engaged recently.

Purpose: To assess your level of protecting behavior.

- ❑ I have asked for help from clergy, police, or lawyers to get my addicted loved one out of an addiction-related criminal charge.
- ❑ I have told friends that I can't come to a social function with a false excuse, when in fact it was due to my addicted loved one's behavior.
- ❑ I have made excuses for my addicted loved one's failure to follow through on personal or professional obligations.
- ❑ I have paid my addicted loved one's bills or other financial obligations even though he was actively using substances.
- ❑ I have loaned money to my addicted loved one to pay the bills he neglected to pay.
- ❑ I have borrowed money from others to pay my addicted loved one's bills.
- ❑ I have called in sick to work for my addicted loved one.
- ❑ I have provided an excuse for her absence when she failed to come home.
- ❑ I have made emotional excuses for my addicted loved one's addiction, such as "He had a tough childhood."
- ❑ I have denied that he, in fact, has an addiction.
- ❑ I have drunk alcohol or used with my addicted loved one even after I was concerned about the issue.
- ❑ I have minimized, rationalized, or justified the actions of my addicted loved one by believing her stories even when my instincts told me she was lying.
- ❑ I have taken over my addicted loved one's responsibilities.

- ❑ I have sidestepped discussing any problems with my addicted loved one.
- ❑ I have avoided my addicted loved one and made excuses to stay away from home rather than admit that he is making home uncomfortable for me.
- ❑ I have purchased drugs or alcohol for my addicted loved one.
- ❑ I have put my addicted loved one to bed and have failed to mention it to him the next day.
- ❑ I have lied to parents, friends, or other family members about my addicted loved one's crises.
- ❑ I have kept my addicted loved one's behavior a secret from people close to me.
- ❑ I have listened without comment to him whine about the unfairness of life.
- ❑ I have bought my addicted loved one things to make her happy so she won't use.
- ❑ I have bailed her out of jail.
- ❑ I have reminded my addicted loved one to eat, to sleep, and to perform other basic activities.
- ❑ I have allowed him to aim disrespectful language at me.

[End exercise 5.1]

[Begin exercise 5.2]

Exercise 5.2: What Protecting Teaches

Refer to the checked boxes in the previous exercise to complete the first sentence in each set of sentences below and then explain what your behavior taught your loved one by completing the second sentence in the set.

Purpose: To recognize that your behavior does not operate in a vacuum.

Example: "One of the ways I protected addiction was <u>I took over Janie's responsibilities.</u> That behavior taught my loved one <u>that she didn't really have responsibilities and that I would make sure we all stayed afloat.</u>

One of the ways I protected addiction was

_____.

That behavior taught my loved one

_____.

One of the ways I protected addiction was

_____.

That behavior taught my loved one

_____.

One of the ways I protected addiction was

_____.

That behavior taught my loved one

_____.

[End exercise 5.2]

In order to be able to stop protecting, you need to understand that there may be more to why you are protecting than simply a desire to save your loved one. In other words, your protecting behavior may not be as well-intentioned as you think.

You may be operating from unconscious motivations that have a payoff for you beyond solely helping your addicted loved one. For example, you may protect in order to control your loved one's behavior. Similarly, your protecting behavior may be based on unwise or incorrect beliefs, illusions or desires. For example, you may believe that your love alone will make your loved one well.

Before you can change any long-standing behavior you must be honest about why you act the way you do and recognize that you will be resistant to change. When you operate from unconscious motivations it is easier to continue old behavior and to wring your hands than it is to leave the comfort of old behavior behind. So ask yourself: *What is my payoff for my behavior?*

[Begin exercise 5.3]

Exercise 5.3: Why I Protect
Check the boxes in Part 1 next to possible payoffs for your protecting behavior and in Part 2 next to how you would feel if you stopped protecting.

Purpose: To evaluate your motivations, which are internal obstacles to change.

Part 1. I protect my addicted loved one because:

- ❑ My self-esteem is boosted by saving the day.
- ❑ I feel needed.
- ❑ My protecting reinforces the fact that I am right.
- ❑ I get a feeling of power.
- ❑ I feel like I have control over my addicted loved one and his addiction.
- ❑ I ensure that my relationship with my addicted loved one will continue.
- ❑ I get a lot of praise. Example: "You are such a good mother/father."
- ❑ By focusing on others I avoid focusing on the problems in my life.
- ❑ I avoid the anger and resentment of my addicted loved one.
- ❑ My protecting adds drama to my life.
- ❑ My protecting produces guilt in my addicted loved one; so maybe she will change.

Part 2. If I stopped protecting, I would feel:

- ❑ Scared
- ❑ Mean
- ❑ Unloving
- ❑ Vindictive
- ❑ Powerful
- ❑ Relieved
- ❑ Uneasy

[End exercise 5.3]

Like unconscious motivations, your beliefs, illusions and desires may guide your protecting behavior. You must become rigorously honest about the underpinnings of your behavior in order to be successful in supporting your loved one's recovery.

[Begin exercise 5.4]

Exercise 5.4: I Believe
Check the boxes next to the statements that reflect what you believe.

Purpose: To identify the beliefs and illusions that may underlie your behavior.

- ❑ I can control my addicted loved one's use.
- ❑ If I love her, she will get well.
- ❑ If my addicted loved one is "happy," he will get well.
- ❑ Struggle is harmful.
- ❑ Everyone needs a life crutch.
- ❑ We are all doing the best we can.
- ❑ We should all help others as often as we can.
- ❑ Saving my addicted loved one from the consequences is helpful.
- ❑ It is loving to rescue others.
- ❑ It is loving to save others from struggle.
- ❑ My addicted loved one just needs a leg up and she can conquer this.
- ❑ All she needs is a job.
- ❑ All my addicted loved one needs is a girlfriend.
- ❑ All he needs are some good friends.
- ❑ All my addicted loved one needs is a little break in life.
- ❑ It is unloving not to answer the phone.
- ❑ It is unloving to withhold money.
- ❑ It is unloving to distrust my addicted loved one.
- ❑ It is unloving to talk to others about our problems.
- ❑ I will know if my addicted loved one is lying.
- ❑ I can in some way control what she does.
- ❑ My addicted loved one's life is now ruined.
- ❑ She will never have love.

[End exercise 5.4]

The Value of Pain

Loving an addict or alcoholic is counterintuitive. Allowing your addicted loved one to suffer seems counterproductive. You wonder: *Isn't addiction a response to pain? Won't allowing my addicted loved one to feel pain encourage further drug use? Why is it so important for him to experience the painful consequences of his behavior?*

The number one reason an addict needs to experience the painful consequences of addiction is that pain and struggle teach a brain deluded by addiction that the costs of addiction outweigh the pleasure of drugs or the benefits of numbness. For your addicted loved one, the pull of drugs may be so extreme that circumstances may need to get really painful before the painful events become enlightening. If using drugs or alcohol is a slice of heaven where pain, misery, disappointment, and insecurity disappear, why stop? The only reason would be because, left to run its natural course, addiction causes such uncomfortable or painful consequences, physically, emotionally, socially and/or spiritually.

If you ease the pain of your loved one's addiction, you likely are diminishing her motivation to accept help and to change. Even when she is in a treatment program or in recovery, you must still let her experience whatever pain arises.

Pain teaches all of us valuable life lessons. "I am often in the position of encouraging parents to back off and let their kids experience all the feelings of the healing process" states Laura Kiley, LCSW, founder and CEO of Inner Harbor for Women, LLC, Tequesta, FL. Laura adds, "We get so uncomfortable watching others in discomfort that we unwittingly interrupt what can be a truly enlightening moment."

Case Study: Declan

Declan and Anna attended one of my family healing workshops with their daughter Leslie while their son John, then age 24, was in treatment for his addiction to prescription drugs. Anna and Leslie were animated during the day while Declan sat stock still with tears in his eyes. Pain radiated from him. Declan later said to me, "It dawned on me for the first time that day that the way I loved John was actually harming him. I learned that I needed to do it differently."

The prime nurturer in the family, Declan was John's safety net and best friend during his insecure school years. Declan made sure that John never felt alone nor suffered consequences for any poor judgment. Although beautifully intentioned, their friendship ultimately crossed the line from nurturing John to protecting John's addiction.

After that first workshop, Declan made huge changes in the way he interacted with John. John later said to me, "My dad did a 180 when he met you. . . . You ruined my life in some ways. We used to be such good friends."

Watching John struggle and not stepping in to ease his discomfort was uncomfortable for Declan. He realized, however, that his instinct to rescue John from the lessons he sorely needed to learn was actually interfering with John's recovery.

Now, John has done the 180. He lives in a sober environment, works, supports his children, attends to his recovery and is heading towards adulthood.

Promoting Happiness Is Not the Same as Promoting Recovery

Like most people, you want your loved ones to be happy, but, like some people, you may ignore the reality that happiness is impossible all of the time. So you may try to avert unhappiness for your addicted loved one by buying things for him, making excuses for him, and ignoring his bad behavior to avoid conflict. As a result, you may be harming him, especially because he is wired to equate happiness with substance use or he finds happiness elusive due to his unrealistic expectations.

By promoting happiness as the goal, you may be creating an impossible standard. Recovery teaches that happiness cannot be the goal; it must be a by-product of living a life with integrity, purpose and meaning.

Case Study: Laura and John

Laura is a social worker and John is a professor. Laura and John reared their son Mark and his younger sister Sarah in upstate New York. The family lived in an idyllic, culturally rich town and traveled extensively. Mark thrived. Sarah, however, had a more difficult time.

Described as anxious from birth, Sarah was socially awkward and overweight, and she possessed an alternative and creative world view. In eighth grade, Sarah discovered that alcohol and pot made her social awkwardness temporarily vanish, and, by her senior year, Sarah felt unable to attend any social function without drinking. Sensing their daughter's fragility, Laura and John sent Sarah to therapists and psychiatrists, and she was prescribed several medications to alleviate her anxiety symptoms.

During her sophomore year of college, Sarah's drug and alcohol use escalated to the point that it was interfering with the benefits of the psychiatric medications. She was no longer able to function. She was barely able to get out of bed and go to class, let alone focus in class. Concerned, Laura and John moved her out of her apartment on campus and back into their house. A few weeks later, Laura called me for help.

Laura, John and I met in their beautiful, sunlit home, which was filled with Navajo rugs, African art, and comfortable furniture. In the family room, Sarah was lying on the couch, unkempt and unwashed, with an empty bag of potato chips by her side. While her mother and I discussed therapeutic options for her, Sarah was completely uninvolved. However, she became alert when the discussion turned to residential treatment for her addiction. (She later told me, "I thought you were just one more flaky professional here to discuss my anxiety and depression.")

Sarah loudly protested, denying that she was an addict. Despite her resistance, Laura, John and I continued discussing Sarah's symptoms. We ultimately agreed that she needed to be treated for her drug abuse problem before trying to determine her other psychological issues.

Sarah adamantly refused to go to drug counseling, and Laura and John listened respectfully and buckled under the pressure. They agreed to confer with Sarah's psychiatrist about the matter, and, if he thought it was necessary, they would enroll Sarah in an outpatient treatment program.

Two weeks later, Laura and John realized that their approach was not working. Sarah was not happier, and her drug use seemed to have escalated again. She stole from them, and, instead of being quietly doped up, she now was angry and aggressive.

Laura explained to me what had happened at the psychiatrist's office. "Sarah wouldn't let us go in with her. But when she came out she told us that her doctor had diagnosed her with ADHD and that he had prescribed Adderall so that she could focus better. The next few days were great. She got out of bed, showered, and went to school. Midway through the second week of school, however, things went haywire. Her mood fluctuated between effusive and chatty and rueful and vicious." Sobbing, Laura said, "I don't think I can live with this anymore."

"You and John have done a lovely job of creating a comfortable home for her, but unfortunately it is also comfortable for her addiction." I responded. "There are absolutely no consequences for her drug use. Why would she stop?" I asked.

"So what kind of consequences are you talking about?" Laura asked. We discussed all the ways Laura and John protected Sarah's addiction by preventing Sarah from experiencing uncomfortable consequences. They paid Sarah's overdraft charges, fixed her car because she couldn't maintain a job, gave her an allowance when she was lying on the couch all day, and allowed her to smoke pot in their home. Also, Laura prepared all of Sarah's meals, did her laundry, and performed all other household tasks for her despite the fact that Sarah was home most of the day and Laura worked.

"When we lay it all out there I guess I do see why nothing is changing. Pretty cushy life she has, huh?" Laura responded in a wry tone.

The next day we all met again. This time, Laura, John, and I laid out a plan for Sarah. There would be no more money for Sarah unless it was to be used for finding a job; no more use of their car if she did not test clean for drugs; no more free ride at home; and no more smoking pot in their home.

Sarah screamed, stomped and wailed in response. She cursed and hissed and stormed out of the house, slamming the door on her way out. Laura and John were stunned.

A few minutes later, Sarah stormed back in to the room to see "if they were thinking more reasonably." This was a different Sarah. Trying to bargain for more privileges, she was calm and logical. When Laura and John held firm, however, she quickly lost her reasonable facade. Again she stomped out of the house.

Sarah returned again a couple of minutes later, this time in tears. Laura and John began to waver. They had been able to persist in the face of Sarah's bullying and placating, but they were almost hopeless in the face of her misery. Yet they held firm. By the end of the meeting, Sarah agreed to go to treatment.

Now, two years later, Sarah is an active member of her recovery community.

The Hurdle of Entitlement

The most stubborn cases of addiction happen when the addict or alcoholic believes that all of his desires will be fulfilled without any obligation on his part. When addiction is combined with entitlement and/or unlimited finances or power, it can spiral out of control quickly and with less pain and fewer enlightening repercussions. Wealth and power can insulate the addict or alcoholic from the pressures of addiction and the need for sobriety.

Entitlement, however, is not limited to the wealthy. Many people in a variety of economic circumstances have reported that they taught their addicted loved ones to expect gratification of their demands and dreams without asserting any effort.

Case Study: Olivia

Olivia and her sister Eliza were born into an upper-class Greenwich, Connecticut family. Always bright, rebellious, and charming, Eliza skated through boarding school with little effort. Boredom and the endless search for novel fun constantly accompanied her. She knew she had not earned all of her gifts; they were hers at birth. But also hers at birth was a genetic predisposition for addiction.

By high school, Eliza was snorting heroin and cocaine in addition to smoking pot daily. Drugs quieted her searching mind and provided a diversion from a life already made dull by the lack of struggle.

Given her unlimited resources, Eliza was a "highly functioning addict." She could snort heroin upon waking in the morning, go to class, snort some heroin again later, and maintain a fairly high grade point average. Even this level of using, however, became routine and boring to Eliza. As her tolerance grew, so did her quest for a bigger and better high.

By her senior year in college, Eliza began using heroin and cocaine intravenously. She spent days on end doing drugs without leaving her house. Her appearance deteriorated due to a lack of sleep and proper nutrition. She stopped showering and her once curly hair had become a rat's nest. None of her "friends" called her parents or notified the school about how sick she was. Instead, they watched her decline while they did her drugs.

Eventually, Olivia became alarmed by Eliza's refusal to answer Olivia's calls or to visit her. One day, Olivia stopped by Eliza's house unannounced and saw the truth. As Olivia recounted later, "I knocked on the door for what felt like hours, and Eliza finally peeked out. For the first time in our lives, she refused to let me come in her place."

After a heated discussion at the threshold, Eliza finally let Olivia come in the house. What she saw was alarming; the house was filthy, and IV needles littered the tables. Olivia knew of Eliza's snorting, but Eliza's current condition was much worse than Olivia had anticipated. She begged Eliza to go to treatment and Eliza cried. Hours later, after eliciting a promise from Eliza to go to treatment, Olivia left and began to research different programs.

When Olivia returned to Eliza's house to take her to the treatment center, Eliza was gone. Olivia was scared but undeterred and hired a private investigator to find Eliza. Once Eliza was found, Olivia bullied her into accepting help.

During the six weeks of Eliza's stay in treatment, Olivia visited her often. However, neither of their parents drove the hour to see Eliza; both explained that they were just too busy.

Eliza left treatment feeling resentful and fully resistant to following any aftercare plan. "She thinks she can do this on her own," Olivia explained to me ruefully. "And my parents are so intent on keeping this whole mess a secret that they are supporting her position. What odds do you give her?" I was thinking Eliza's odds were lousy, but then I remembered that I had seen miracles with less hope and told Olivia so.

Eliza flew under the radar for a couple of months. She went back to school, re-enrolled in the classes she had failed, kicked out her roommates, and began collecting money from the family trust fund. She claimed she was no longer doing heroin or other "big" drugs, but she had reverted to daily marijuana use. She lied and told Olivia that, because weed was not her problem, the treatment center had told her she could still use it.

After a couple of months, in a fit of restless boredom, Eliza began snorting heroin. Her tolerance was too high for snorting to provide pleasure for long and, within two months, she was back to a daily IV heroin habit.

At this point, Olivia hired a lawyer to institute legal proceedings to have Eliza declared incompetent and to have family trust fund distributions to her restricted to times when she was sober, as determined by an addiction professional. Eliza ignored the summons and did not show up at the competency hearing.

The first consequence for Eliza arrived in the form of a registered letter letting her know that no more money would be forthcoming until she provided a hair sample revealing that she was not using drugs. Eliza refused to provide the sample and soon had an empty checking account.

When the money ran out, Eliza began calling her parents. Despite Olivia's and the lawyer's coaching, Eliza's parents, long on money and short on patience and fortitude, gave her money each time she called, depositing a few hundred dollars for "food" into her account.

Olivia soon found out and had an angry discussion with her parents. For the next few weeks, they refused to take Eliza's calls. Undeterred, Eliza showed up in person, full of rage and recriminations. She told them it was their fault she was an addict. They caved in, gave her a check, and ushered her out of their house.

Olivia called me again, this time in tears. "My parents mean well but they just don't get it. They aren't strong enough or savvy enough or introspective enough to handle this. What can I do?"

I encouraged Olivia to address her parents' protecting behavior with them again. Olivia begged her parents to stop the flow of funds. In a moment of honest insight, they agreed to hire a "money boss" whose sole function would be to act as a firewall between Eliza and her parents.

The next time Eliza called her parents for money she was informed about the new system. Furious, she called Olivia. "You are ruining my life," she screamed.

Olivia calmly replied, "No, I am trying to keep you alive."

Ultimately, Eliza reentered treatment and embraced recovery. It took some effort on her family's part, but Eliza had learned that a life of privilege did not give her a free pass to be an addict.

Chapter 6   Codependency

"How empty of me, to be so full of you." ~Anonymous

Addiction is described as a family disease because family members experience the chaos and dysfunction of addiction while their addicted loved one is too numb to experience it. They live in a chronic state of stress and can become ill. As their loved one gets sicker, they start organizing their lives around attempting to avoid the chaos that accompanies active addiction.

It is not uncommon for family members to suffer wide-ranging physical and psychological damage. Their neural structures have changed. Where once their thoughts were centered on the future and their goals, their thoughts now turn to rescuing their addicted loved one.

A common term for this loss of self-focus is "codependency." As described by Sarah Allen Benton, MS, LMHC, addiction clinician and author of *Understanding the High-Functioning Alcoholic*, "One family member's addiction can infiltrate the entire family dynamic. Therefore it is equally important for parents of addicted loved ones to access resources and to begin their own healing process."

There are numerous characteristics and symptoms of codependency. If you find yourself behaving or feeling as described below, you may need to seek help:

- Your self-esteem is dependent upon pleasing and controlling others.
- You assume another's responsibilities at the expense of your own needs.
- Your primary coping mechanism is denial.
- You are depressed.

- You are constantly on guard and are waiting for the other shoe to drop.
- You engage in compulsive behavior to ease your stress.
- You are living with constant anxiety.
- You are struggling with a stress-related illness.
- You have remained in a current relationship with an active addict or alcoholic for too long without seeking outside help.

Codependency does not operate in a vacuum. When all of the energy and resources in a family or a relationship are devoted to the needs of only one person, the other(s) in the family or relationship are diminished. This generally results in additional dysfunction and increased resentment.

[Begin exercise 6.1]

Exercise 6.1: Characteristics of Codependency
Check the boxes next to the statements about you that apply most of the time.

Purpose: To reflect upon your behavior that may be considered codependent.

- ❑ I anticipate my addicted loved one's needs.
- ❑ I feel safest emotionally when giving to my addicted loved one.
- ❑ My good feelings about myself stem from being liked by others.
- ❑ My addicted loved one's struggle affects my serenity.
- ❑ Most of my attention revolves around solving my addicted loved one's problems.
- ❑ I assume responsibility for the thoughts of my addicted loved one.
- ❑ I assume responsibility for the actions of my addicted loved one.
- ❑ I assume responsibility for the destiny of my addicted loved one.
- ❑ I feel guilty when my addicted loved one has a problem.
- ❑ I feel anxious when my addicted loved one has a problem.
- ❑ I feel compelled to solve problems for my addicted loved one.
- ❑ I have few interests of my own separate from my family members' interests.
- ❑ I put my needs last.
- ❑ I drop whatever I am doing and come to my addicted loved one's rescue.
- ❑ I feel angry and frustrated if my solutions don't solve my addicted loved one's problems.
- ❑ I do things for my family members that they are capable of doing for themselves.
- ❑ I feel my addicted loved one's pain more than I feel my own.
- ❑ I have a very limited social life separate from my family members.

- One of my primary ways of coping is to deny painful realities about my addicted loved one.
- I feel a sense of satisfaction if my addicted loved one follows my advice.
- I have become addicted to controlling my addicted loved one's decisions.
- I have difficulty expressing my feelings.
- I tend to react to my addicted loved one's requests instead of thinking calmly and reaching my own decisions.
- I am a perfectionist and judge myself harshly.
- My sense of self-worth is derived from the good opinions of others about me and my behavior.
- I find it difficult to be vulnerable and to ask for help.
- I am extremely loyal, even when it is unjustified.
- It seems like I always have chaos and crisis in my life.
- My sense of self-worth comes from being needed by my addicted loved one.
- I am unselfish and tend to always be giving to someone.
- I mask pain with humor, isolation, and anger.
- I have difficulty accepting praise from others.
- When my good deeds go unrecognized, I feel bad about myself.
- My mental attention is focused on pleasing others.
- My mental attention is focused on protecting others.
- My mental attention is focused on getting others to see things my way or to solve problems my way.
- My self-esteem is bolstered by solving my addicted loved one's problems.
- My self-esteem is bolstered by relieving another's pain.

- ❑ My addicted loved one's appearance is a reflection on me.
- ❑ My addicted loved one's struggle with addiction is a reflection on my parenting.
- ❑ My fears of being rejected by my addicted loved one dictate my decisions.
- ❑ I am not really aware of how I feel, only how my addicted loved one feels.

[End exercise 6.1]

[Begin exercise 6.2]

Exercise 6.2: Do I Need Help?

Check the boxes next to your thoughts and behavior on a regular basis.

Purpose: To assess your need for specialized codependency support services or groups.

- ❑ I lie awake at night because I am worrying about my addicted loved one's drug or alcohol use.
- ❑ I am having trouble concentrating at work because I am worrying.
- ❑ I walk on egg shells at home trying to keep my addicted loved one happy.
- ❑ I often monitor my addicted loved one's use.
- ❑ I avoid social situations where alcohol is available.
- ❑ I am embarrassed by the substance-abuse-related behavior of my addicted loved one.
- ❑ I think that I imagine that my addicted loved one is using more than she is.
- ❑ I am repeatedly disappointed when I am proven wrong about my addicted loved one's drug or alcohol use.
- ❑ I feel isolated or alienated from my addicted loved one.
- ❑ I have mood swings ranging from elation to depression for no apparent reason.
- ❑ I feel anger at my addicted loved one that seems unprovoked.
- ❑ I minimize to myself and others my addicted loved one's use.
- ❑ I protect my addicted loved one from the consequences of his use.
- ❑ I feel pity for my addicted loved one and make excuses for her with "outsiders."
- ❑ I am gaining or losing weight.
- ❑ I am suffering from anxiety attacks.

- [ ] I have a constant knot in my stomach.
- [ ] I no longer feel like having sex.
- [ ] I have sex even when I don't want to do so.
- [ ] I am isolating myself from my friends.
- [ ] I don't discuss my problems with my friends because I am too embarrassed.
- [ ] I have taken on all the jobs my addicted loved one used to do.
- [ ] I have become the super-parent to protect my children.
- [ ] I overreact to small infractions with all of my children.
- [ ] I have assumed all responsibility for financial matters that rightly should be in the hands of my addicted loved one.
- [ ] My social life is diminishing.
- [ ] The quality of my life is in direct relationship to the quality of my addicted loved one's life.
- [ ] I am struggling with depression.
- [ ] I am hyper-vigilant about all the details of my addicted loved one's life.
- [ ] I am drinking alcohol or using other drugs to calm myself more than in the past.
- [ ] I struggle with headaches.
- [ ] I struggle with high blood pressure.
- [ ] I have insomnia.
- [ ] I have panic attacks.
- [ ] My memory is impaired.
- [ ] I am struggling with a stress-related medical disorder.

[End exercise 6.2]

Case Study: Patricia

"Joseph needs help, and we are so scared," said Patricia to me about her 45-year-old son. "He is a talented boy and is ruining his life. He is destroying his business, and he speaks rudely to me. I don't know what to do." With each sentence, Patricia's voice got a little shriller and her European accent more pronounced.

Patricia's daughter Niki interrupted and explained, "We are not sure when Joseph started using meth, but over the last five years he has gotten more and more bizarre. Several times he has wound up in the psych ward because of his delusional thinking, and he has been arrested twice. Each time he goes on a meth binge, he destroys his room looking for nonexistent listening devices. At the end of each hospitalization, the doctors recommend residential treatment, medicate him, and then release him. They think he has bipolar disorder and that these crazy episodes are triggered by his meth use."

Patricia wailed, "He is going to die!"

"We have tried everything to get Joseph to see a psychiatrist," Niki continued. "We've tried to get him to take care of himself, but he is in a really bad pattern. He goes a little or a lot crazy, we get him hospitalized, he gets out, and he behaves okay for a few weeks or months, but eventually he goes back to using drugs and then the cycle starts all over. After his most recent hospitalization, Joseph agreed to go to residential treatment. We were thrilled. Twenty-four hours later, however, Joseph left the hospital and came to Mom's house. I begged her to not let him come home but she just can't say no."

This last piece of the pattern is a crucial part of Joseph's cycle. Joseph comes home; Patricia becomes the nurse and caretaker and assumes responsibility for his mental health. Joseph assumes little of the responsibility for his own care, and he remains uncommitted to recovery.

On the surface, Patricia's behavior seems selflessly loving. As I later learned, however, Patricia's actions are in part motivated by her desire to avert the anxiety and depression she experiences when Joseph is out of sight. She also avoids the well of loneliness she lived with before he became sick.

Chapter 7   Healthy Boundaries

One of the most effective tools to address codependency is to develop healthy boundaries. Boundaries are the imaginary lines that separate your needs, wants, dreams, opinions, and emotions from those of another person. Healthy boundaries can be hard to maintain in any family or household. But when someone in the family or household is an addict or alcoholic, everyone else needs to be extra vigilant.

Establishing healthy emotional barriers between you and your addicted loved one is crucial for you and him. Boundaries protect you, guard your heart from unrealistic hopes, and keep you from engaging in "protecting" behavior. Boundaries also help to expedite your addicted loved one's progression from using to recovery.

The purpose of boundaries is to keep the chaos of addiction outside of you and to preserve your love for the addict or alcoholic. For example, if your boundaries fail and you give into your addicted loved one's manipulations or allow him to disrespect you, your natural resentment may endanger the love you feel for him. Healthy boundaries protect you and your loved one from engaging in a dance that ultimately damages the love you and he have for each other.

Case Study: Sally

Sally, a mother of three from a small southern town, called me frantic with worry about her 22-year-old son Burton. As described by Sally, Burton alternated between periods of cocaine use and periods of bulimia. When using cocaine, he didn't eat or sleep for days. When he ran out of drugs, he binge ate and purged, gorging himself on cookies and snack foods and then throwing up in the bucket he kept by his bed. Burton routinely went through weeks of no eating followed by weeks of gorging and purging.

"He is 6 feet tall and weighs only 110 pounds," said Sally. "His hair is lifeless, his skin is starting to look dry and grey, and he looks so sick I am just sure he is going to have a heart attack and die."

I recommended an intervention and Sally agreed. A few days later, Sally, Burton's father, brother, and sister, and I met in a hotel meeting room to prepare for the intervention, which was scheduled for the next day in the family's home. During that meeting, Burton's family members expressed revulsion about his bulimia mixed with anger about his rude behavior and its impact on their family.

"It's just gross," said Burton's younger brother Mike. "Mom buys all this great food, and he sneaks it up to our room. I hear the crackle of packages opening and then I hear him eating as if he can't get the food in his mouth fast enough. A few minutes after that I hear him puking. The smell makes me gag. He is so disgusting. He sleeps with that bucket next to his bed and spends all night eating and puking. I like it better when he is using coke—at least he doesn't gross me out."

Burton's younger sister Ashley was stony. "I don't want to be here. Every conversation we have in this family is about *him*."

I asked Burton's parents about their boundaries should he refuse our help. "So what action are you willing to take if he refuses treatment? Words are lovely but they need to be backed up by new action or it's just more talk."

"I am unwilling to go on anymore as if everything is okay," replied Sally. "We need help and I am going to ask for it." Sally proceeded to read from a piece of paper she had been holding tightly in her hand:

Notice: If you see Burton Green please tell him that he needs help. He is a cocaine addict and a bulimic and I am sure he is going to die if he won't accept professional help. If you have any compassion for him, and the rest of our family, please do not ignore the situation. We his family need your help.
Signed, Sally Green

"What do you intend to do with that?" I asked.

"I am going to publish it in our local paper if he refuses to go to treatment. If I am going to be printing an obituary soon, then I might as well print something that might help first," Sally said with absolute resolve.

Early the next morning the intervention began. Assembled in the living room were Burton's parents, grandparents, and siblings and me. Burton came downstairs and turned around on his heels when he saw us sitting there quietly. His father strong-armed him back into the room and he grudgingly sat down.

Burton's father, grandparents, and siblings read their intervention letters expressing clear concern and love both in their words and in their voices. Burton sat through the reading of those letters as if he were made of stone; his only words, said in an expressionless voice, were "You are all crazy. I don't need help."

Sally then read her letter and handed Burton the notice she intended to publish. He looked at the piece of paper and said, "What ####### is this?" Everyone in the room gasped at the obscenity he used. Sally calmly told Burton what she had told me about publishing the notice.

"You are crazy. You would never do this. You care too much what everyone in town will say," Burton said defiantly.

"Watch me," Sally responded. She got up from the couch, grabbed the phone, and dialed a number. "Classifieds, please." After a moment, she continued, "This is Sally Green and I am interested in taking out a full page ad as soon as possible."

Burton levitated off the couch, grabbed the receiver, and hung up the phone. All the fight gone, Burton packed his bag without any more resistance.

Love That Protects Everyone

After you have tried multiple times to have reasonable conversations with your addicted loved one about your concerns, you may well realize your old patterns of interacting just are not working. Your loved one remains sick and you are getting sick, too. This is one of the toughest crossroads. Do you continue with the same behavior and hope she will see the light? Or, if she will not change, will you change?

If you opt for change and create healthy boundaries, you will begin to engage in behavior that truly protects your addicted loved one as well as the whole family. If you once saw love as a kind and sweet emotion, you will begin to realize love may be a little saltier, tougher, and assertive. And, contrary to your old way of thinking, you realize that it may be loving to:

- Let your addicted loved one sit in jail when bailing her out is likely to lead to her continued drug use.
- Kick her out of your home if being there helps her evade the consequences of her drug use.
- Call child services if a minor is in your addicted loved one's care.
- Take your addicted loved one to a shelter if he left treatment early.
- Let him bury himself in debt instead of bailing him out.

- Watch your addicted loved one lose job after job without offering her financial assistance.

- Limit your financial support of her to her treatment expenses.

Although healthy boundaries are specific to the person and the situation, some boundaries are universally healthy or unhealthy. In essence, healthy boundaries allow a person to control what is within his purview and only that. As Charles Rubin stated in *Don't Let Your Kids Kill You, 3d Ed.*:

> The only control parents have is over their own actions and reactions. How you deal with your own emotions makes all the difference. You can continue to be a victim to what is essentially an insane situation due to the chemicals your children are using, or you can control the situation through the setting of boundaries, making a conscious effort not to allow your addicts to intrude upon you.

Signs of unhealthy boundaries (or no boundaries) include:
- Trusting no one or everyone with personal information;
- Talking about intimate subjects in social situations with strangers;
- Giving someone else power over your decisions; and
- Expecting others to read your mind.

Signs of healthy boundaries include:
- Revealing yourself a little at a time;
- Staying focused on your own growth and recovery;
- Determining your own values and opinions;
- Respecting others' opinions and boundaries; and
- Trusting your own intuition.

[Begin exercise 7.1]

Exercise 7.1: Boundary Confusion
Check the boxes next to behaviors that you engage in often.

Purpose: To help you determine where your boundaries are vulnerable.

- ☑ I clean up messes in my home that <u>others</u> create.
- ☑ I give advice without being asked.
- ☑ I judge others when their opinions differ from mine.
- ☐ I make decisions about vacations without consulting others.
- ☑ I tend to offer solutions while someone is discussing her problems.
- ☐ I listen to others long past the time a conversation needs to end.
- ☑ I am reluctant to be the person who hangs up the phone first.
- ☑ Even if I am busy, I make myself available when the phone rings.
- ☐ I get angry or hurt when someone says no to me.
- ☑ I want to know all of my child's secrets.
- ☑ When a question is asked of someone else, I answer for him.
- ☑ I rescue others from the consequences of their choices.
- ☐ In a restaurant I let someone else order for me.
- ☐ In a restaurant I order for others.
- ☑ I look for friendship from my children.
- ☐ I call professionals by their first name without invitation.
- ☐ I sometimes find myself wanting to be nurtured by my child.
- ☑ I feel put upon when someone asks me for a favor.
- ☐ I talk to people in a subordinate position at work about my problems.
- ☐ I allow others to blame me for their problems.
- ☐ I take the blame for a situation to save someone else discomfort.
- ☐ I find that people say inappropriate things to me, and I remain silent.
- ☐ I disclose very personal information in inappropriate settings.

[End exercise 7.1]

Case Study: Elena and Chuck

"I was given your name by Martha [an admissions coordinator for a local treatment center]," a weary female voice said to me when I answered the phone. "Our son David is using heroin, and I don't know what to do."

David's mother Elena proceeded to describe David's manipulations for money, his history of erratic behavior, his deteriorating school performance, and the continual efforts of Elena and her husband Chuck to pick up the pieces of David's life. She went on to explain that David was in complete denial and refused all help despite being in the middle of a disciplinary proceeding at college for possession of drugs.

I suggested an intervention and explained what an intervention would involve and could accomplish. "That's exactly what we need to do," said Elena, her voice now filled with something approaching hope.

Over the next few days, I spoke daily with Elena and Chuck. I learned that they were the kind of people everybody wants for parents—caring yet genuinely committed to making tough changes. I thought: *If addiction can happen in this family, it can happen to anybody.* I've said that about other families in the past, always secretly hoping I was wrong. But it is true. Over and over, I have witnessed kids raised in the healthiest of families fall prey to addiction.

The following week, Elena, Chuck, David's older sister Hannah and younger brother Thomas, and I gathered in David's college counselor's office to prepare for the intervention we had scheduled for later that morning. We talked about David's drug history. Hannah and Thomas possessed a lot more information than their parents, and both siblings cried with concern for their brother. Then, all four of them wrote intervention statements, outlining what they knew about David's drug use, how worried they were about him, the changes they had observed in him, and what boundaries they were going to put in place if he refused treatment.

Next, we all sat waiting with anxiety for David to arrive. Eventually, after what felt like hours, David came into the office. The intervention went without a hitch. Each family member expressed loving concern, some of them in tears, and David agreed to go to treatment even though he professed no need for it.

Elena and Chuck were thrilled and shocked. They thought David would be much more resistant. I was not surprised given the statistic that professionally facilitated interventions are successful between 85 to 90 percent of the time; David was in the majority.

After detox and a 28-day stint in residential treatment, David wanted to come home. Even though it was early in their journey, Elena and Chuck were too savvy to agree. They were prophetically concerned that David's struggle toward recovery was too easily won.

Elena and Chuck offered continuing support for David by agreeing to pay for a sober residence or further treatment, as recommended by the treatment professionals, but they jointly and firmly refused David's repeated requests to move home. I cheered for them on the sidelines.

Ultimately, David agreed to go to sober housing and packed up his things, complete with bottles of "clean urine" that he, in a premeditative mindset, had accumulated while clean and sober in the treatment facility. He moved to a sober house, relapsed, and used his stored clean urine to fake the urine tests. He was ultimately caught and kicked out of the house. Chuck and

Elena refused to let him come home and reiterated their previous stance; they would pay for sober housing or treatment, but home was not an option.

Elena and Chuck took all the right steps, read voraciously about addiction and their roles in the equation, and became part of an Al-Anon group, but David just was not playing ball. Over the five-month period following his relapse, he accumulated the consequences of a drug life, including arrests, overdoses, evictions, and homeless "couch surfing."

Elena and Chuck steadfastly allowed David to experience each of those consequences. David's struggles changed them, but did not embitter them. Instead, they became imbued with an awe-inspiring resolve.

When I first met them, Elena and Chuck could have been classified as slightly permissive parents. One year later, they had developed boundaries as tight as a drum. Their love prevented them from colluding with David's addiction. They did not bail him out when he was arrested; they did not give him money after he was evicted from the sober house. What Elena and Chuck did was incredibly hard. Saying no to David when he called from jail and no when he wanted money took enormous resolve.

David finally got the message. Now, David is a changed man, active in a Twelve Step fellowship, sponsoring others, and speaking about addiction. Elena and Chuck became better people as well. When I speak with them, they sound grateful and not just because David is doing so well. They are grateful for the changes they underwent as well.

The Four Boundary Questions

For those with little practice in setting boundaries, the exercise of setting boundaries will feel strange at first. It might even feel wrong and scary. To help determine whether creating a new boundary or strengthening an existing boundary is necessary, ask yourself the following questions when faced with a problem:

- *Whose problem is it?* If it is your addicted loved one's problem, give her a chance to solve it.

- *Who will grow from solving the problem?* If your addicted loved one would grow from solving the problem and you solve the problem instead, your loved one misses an opportunity to mature.

- *Who will benefit if I solve the problem?* If your addicted loved would benefit from solving the problem, you would take that opportunity away by solving the problem. Also, if you are always solving everyone else's problems, your life is most likely diminishing.

- *What opportunity will be lost if I solve the problem?* In addition to growing and benefitting, there may be other opportunities for your addicted loved one if he solves the problem. It may be as simple as the opportunity for him to feel good about his success.

Boundaries are at times difficult even for those with the most practice, but boundaries are best learned by doing. So roll up your sleeves and get ready.

The following two exercises are designed to increase your awareness of boundary-crossing behaviors—yours and your addicted loved one's.

[Begin exercise 7.2]

Exercise 7.2: Boundary Tools

Some family members of addicted loved ones find it helpful to make a written list of what they will and will not do. Consider using the ledger below by filling in each box with specific responsibilities. If possible, sit down with your addicted loved one and encourage him to fill in the boxes in his column.

My Responsibilities	Addicted Loved One's Responsibilities
Example: My journey of change	*Example: My recovery*
Example: I am willing to pay for his treatment, but no other expenses.	*Example: I choose to enter 30 days of inpatient treatment.*
Example: He may stay in my home if he is clean and sober and pays rent.	*Example: I am willing to live in my mother's home under her restrictions.*

[End exercise 7.2]

[Begin exercise 7.3]

Exercise 7.3: Boundary Scripting

Imagine you are talking to your addicted loved one and complete the sentences set out below.

Guidelines:
1. *Be specific.*
2. *Be reasonable.*
3. *Make the boundary enforceable.*
4. *Make the boundary logically related to the request or violation.*

Purpose: To practice setting boundaries before a predictable confrontation so as to reduce the chance that you'll get caught off guard and to aid you in thinking reasonably, not reactively, when a confrontation is unexpected.

Examples:
- *I understand that you <u>are in a jam and need a ride home from the bar</u>. I won't do that because <u>you need to solve problems of your making</u>.*
- *I understand that you <u>would like me to loan you some money</u>. I won't do that because <u>there is a possibility that any money I give you will be used for drugs</u>.*

I understand that you _____.

I won't do that because _____

_____.

I understand that you _____.

I won't do that because _____

_____.

I understand that you _____.

I won't do that because _____

_____.

[End exercise 7.3]

Why It Is Hard to Set Boundaries

New boundaries are not often met with applause. In most families, addicted loved ones and, indeed, other family members, accustomed to certain behavior, will become uncomfortable when new boundaries are established. "Testing" behavior is likely to ensue in the form of withdrawal, anger, overt refusal to engage, or passive avoidance.

"The most extreme cases of boundary testing are when this is new parenting conduct," says John Palmer, BSW, Director of Operations at Turning Point, a residential treatment center in New Haven, CT. John adds, "Part of our job is to encourage parents of our residents to set healthy boundaries and then to manage the testing behavior of our residents."

Your boundaries might be tested 10,000 times; it is your job to withstand the assault.

New boundaries may also create internal conflict for you. Anytime a person changes her behavior, the fear that propelled the original behavior is likely to surface. Some common fears that may arise for you when you begin setting boundaries are the following:

- Fear that your addicted loved one will commit suicide.
- Fear that she will overdose.
- Fear that you will never see your addicted loved one again.
- Fear that he will live on the streets.
- Fear that your addicted loved one will turn to prostitution.
- Fear that you are the one responsible for her addiction.
- Fear that your addicted loved one will physically harm you.
- Fear that all you have built will be lost.

These fears are legitimate in the sense that what you fear may actually happen. In my experience, however, it is unlikely that your failure to set boundaries will prevent the consequences that you fear, and it is likely that your setting boundaries will lead your addicted loved one to accept help.

Either way, your loved one's reaction to your boundaries is beyond your control and unpredictable. What is predictable is what will happen if you don't set boundaries. Failure to set boundaries against the chaos of addiction results in harm to you, to other family members, and ultimately to your addicted loved one.

Faced with a continual barrage against your boundaries, you may revert to your old boundaries and attempt to control the situation by trying to control your addicted loved one. I have observed countless people try to control the uncontrollable by engaging in the behaviors listed in the following exercise. Continued reliance on those behaviors without any resultant change on your loved one's part can qualify as insane behavior. As the adage attributed to Albert Einstein states: "The definition of insanity is doing the same thing over and over again and expecting a different result."

[Begin exercise 7.4]

Exercise 7.4: Controlling Behaviors

Check the boxes next to the behaviors you have exhibited with your addicted loved one. Then, for each such behavior, ask, "Did it change the situation in a meaningful way?"

Purpose: To recognize and to assess the effectiveness of your attempts to control another's behavior.

- ❑ Silent treatment
- ❑ Over-functioning
- ❑ Lying
- ❑ Making threats
- ❑ Distributing or doling out substances
- ❑ Placating
- ❑ Assuming responsibilities that are not yours
- ❑ Pretending
- ❑ Lecturing
- ❑ Avoiding
- ❑ Hiding or dumping drugs
- ❑ People pleasing

[End exercise 7.4]

Phase III: Family Healing

The final phase of your journey starts with surrender, incorporates forgiveness and taking care of yourself, brings purpose and meaning to your life, and propels you to be grateful for the gifts your journey has made available to you.

Chapter 8   Surrender

Some family members of addicts or alcoholics are lucky; their loved ones go to treatment, embrace recovery, and make recovery a backdrop to life instead of an ongoing ordeal.   Others, however, are not as lucky; for their loved ones, recovery is more erratic.   Months of sobriety are punctuated with periods of active addiction.

Whatever the situation with your addicted loved one, your constant focus on him has great potential to steal all joy from your life. You will remain worried, scared, and almost paralyzed.   You will have no hope.   You will always be waiting for the other shoe to drop.   Conversely, if you continue your journey of change, progressing from fear to surrender, you likely will discover, or rediscover, at least some joy and peace.

Surrender does not mean losing hope or giving up.   Instead, it is the realization that you cannot and do not control your loved one.   Surrender does not come painlessly.   In fact, those who have been there have told me that it took a stretch of darkness and grief before they gave into surrender. Before the darkness, most considered surrender unimaginable.   After the darkness, they realized that, in the long run, they were not in control of their addicted loved one's addiction or recovery.

Addiction recovery is the addict's or alcoholic's responsibility, a responsibility that will be born (if at all) of her desire to change her life. She has to discover her purpose for recovery, and you have to discover your purpose for your journey.

When you stop trying to control the uncontrollable, you have a great deal more energy to reflect and to find the meaning in the whole ordeal. Through the process of surrender it becomes possible for you to transcend the experience, to reclaim your life, and to live with joy and peace.

[Begin exercise 8.1]

Exercise 8.1: Surrender Assessment
Check the boxes next to the statements that describe you at this time.

Purpose: To assess your level of surrender.

- ❑ If I don't keep up with all that my addicted loved one does, he is likely to relapse.
- ❑ I spend a large portion of each day wondering about my addicted loved one.
- ❑ I often question the decisions of his treatment professionals.
- ❑ I seem to read only about addiction.
- ❑ When I talk to my addicted loved one, I always ask recovery-related questions.
- ❑ When anxious about my addicted loved one's recovery, I immediately pick up the phone and call him.
- ❑ I know the name and number of my addicted loved one's sponsor.
- ❑ I call her treatment center more than once a week.
- ❑ I am always waiting for the other shoe to drop.
- ❑ I believe that I am the only "real" support my addicted loved one has.
- ❑ I am afraid to turn off my cell phone.
- ❑ I am always planning the next treatment for my addicted loved one just in case she relapses.
- ❑ I am suffering from anxiety-related disorders.
- ❑ When I am anxious, I engage in controlling behavior.
- ❑ I often worry about my addicted loved one's happiness.
- ❑ I buy things for my addicted loved one when I am anxious.
- ❑ If I say no to a request by my addicted loved one, I am sure he will relapse.

❑ I have assumed responsibility for his business matters, *e.g.*, paying his bills and taxes.

❑ I have become the recovery police.

❑ I find myself controlling my other loved ones out of fear.

[End exercise 8.1]

Surrendering Expectations

Like many people, you may have climbed out of denial about your loved one's addiction, but still you resist accepting that her recovery requires that you make changes in your life. An addict who embraces recovery rarely goes back to the *status quo* of her pre-recovery days. She has changed her goals, dreams, and desires. And you and other well-meaning family members must change your goals, dreams, and desires for her.

If you fail to accept the changes in your loved one and try to lure her back into a predictable fold, you may be encouraging a negative outcome: relapse and regression. For instance, you may have to accept the fact that your once college-bound child may need an entirely different launching pad in life. Average college life is not realistic for many in the early years of recovery given that dorm life on most college campuses is synonymous with drug and alcohol use. Similarly, some professions are so stress-filled that an outgrowth of recovery must be a career change for your loved one.

Any reluctance you have to give up your dreams for your loved one is understandable. Our culture defines success narrowly: college, career, economic stability, marriage, children, more money, and more stuff. Nonetheless, your loved one on a recovery path may need to abandon these preconceived notions to protect her sobriety.

In addition to your goals, dreams, and desires for your loved one, you must surrender your expectations regarding her recovery. For example, you must let go of any expectation that she will stop needing to go to AA meetings or that she will not tell others about her addiction.

[Begin exercise 8.2]

Exercise 8.2: Surrendering Expectations

Check the boxes next to your goals, dreams, desires and expectations for your addicted loved one.

Purpose: To determine and to evaluate your "agenda" for your loved one.

I expect that my loved one will:

- ☑ Get over this phase.
- ☑ Go to college as planned.
- ☑ Have a professional career.
- ☐ Get married and have children.
- ☐ Follow in the family business or career path.
- ☑ Attend social functions where alcohol is served without its being stressful.
- ☐ Get over the need to participate in AA.
- ☐ Ultimately engage in a "normal" life where addiction is a passing memory.
- ☑ Want to maintain a close connected relationship with me.
- ☐ Be reunited with and stay close to her siblings, who will forgive her.
- ☐ Be different and no longer exhibit personality characteristics that I associate with addiction.
- ☐ Become an active member of my church.
- ☐ Live his adult life in close proximity to me.
- ☑ Surrender resentments against me as soon as he gets sober.
- ☑ Give up her immature patterns of behavior.
- ☐ Not tell others about his addiction.
- ☐ Always struggle with active addiction.
- ☐ Make all her friends from the recovery community.
- ☑ Become a sponsor in a recovery program.

[End exercise 8.2]

Case Study: Coco

I received a phone call from Coco while Clare, her 22-year-old daughter, was in treatment. Coco was interested in attending one of my family healing workshops and she asked what we would be covering. I explained that we would talk about addiction as a disease, the neuroscience of addiction, genetic predisposition, and strategies families can use to stay healthy.

She sort of snickered. "Stay healthy. You mean get healthy." Then she asked, "Do you ever see mothers and daughters becoming close after treatment. Right now, she is so angry at me."

"Give it time," I told her. "You may have a good relationship with her in the future."

Quietly she asked: "If the relationship was always rocky, can it ever really change?"

"True reconciliations happen all the time," I assured her.

Coco went on to explain that she and Clare's father, Mark, had divorced when Clare was a toddler and that Coco and Mark had been engaged in a covert war for Clare's love ever since. Whenever Coco tried to reign in Clare during her middle school and high school years, Clare would call her father, who would contradict Coco. The result was that Clare did whatever she wanted without any enforceable restrictions. She was a teenager without the wisdom or resources for that kind of responsibility, and she made really poor choices. One of those choices was substance abuse, which, over time, led to an addiction to opiates.

I got to know Coco and her current husband Will pretty well over the next few years. Coco worked harder than I would have thought possible. She read books and attended groups and seminars.

Clare, on the other hand, relapsed two months after treatment, although she feigned recovery and told Coco that everything was fine. Instead of pretending with her, Coco continued to seek an honest relationship with her. Clare, however, wanted her mother to ignore her unreliability, lying, and obvious drug use. Clare was often angry with Coco for calling attention to the holes in her stories.

After a couple of years of continuous battling to make Clare see the light, Coco surrendered. Coco now seeks to control only those things over which she has dominion. She has healthy boundaries. She even found a few gifts for herself along the way, such as a renewed faith in a higher power, patience, and compassion for other parents. She considers herself a better person for the struggle.

Today, Coco reaches out to Clare, offers help when it seems like Clare will be receptive, and draws her hand back when Clare scratches. Coco does not bail Clare out of her economic scrapes nor does Coco trust Clare for any reliable contact. They do, however, have moments of joy together and a genuine relationship.

Surrendering Resentments

Another level of surrender that can help you to find or to rediscover joy is letting go of the resentments you may have built up during your loved one's active addiction. After you surrender your resentments, you will be able to build a relationship with your addicted loved one based on respect, empathy, and compassion.

[Begin exercise 8.3]

Exercise 8.3: Harboring Resentments

Check the boxes next to the behaviors and consequences for which you harbor resentments against your addicted loved one.

Purpose: To explore your underlying resentments.

I harbor resentments against my addicted loved one for:

- ❑ Lying to me
- ❑ Manipulating me
- ❑ Stealing from me or others
- ❑ Placating me
- ❑ Bullying me
- ❑ Violating my boundaries
- ❑ Verbally abusing me
- ❑ Destroying property
- ❑ Racking up hospital bills
- ❑ Putting me in the position of having to pay treatment expenses
- ❑ Constantly seeking something from me
- ❑ Displaying poor judgment
- ❑ Embarrassing me
- ❑ Expressing repulsive ideology
- ❑ Flunking out of college
- ❑ Wasting money
- ❑ Taking advantage of my connections in the work world
- ❑ Selling drugs or engaging in other criminal behavior
- ❑ Hurting others I love
- ❑ Treating me and others disrespectfully
- ❑ Destroying my piece of mind
- ❑ Damaging my relationships with others

[End exercise 8.3]

If you are like most people, the real trick is to let go of resentments even when there is no guarantee that your loved one won't continue to engage in offensive behavior. But surrender (and forgiveness) do not depend on the status of your loved one's sobriety. In fact, surrender is the willingness to have a relationship, albeit sometimes limited, regardless of your loved one's use. How vulnerable you make yourself with your loved one depends, in part, on his trustworthiness, but, once you have let go of your resentments, you will see that he is never too sick for empathy, compassion, and love.

Chapter 9   Forgiveness

Forgiveness is more than just words and goes beyond reducing or eliminating resentments. Often, forgiveness requires a good deal of internal work.

One internal block to forgiveness is anger. Possibly, during the days of chaos and crisis, you buried deep within yourself anger at your addicted loved one because there just wasn't the time or the energy to focus on your feelings. Now, even though the days are better, the anger permeates your relationship with her. If so, you must unearth your anger so that you can move beyond it. Then, and only then, can you make a conscious decision to forgive.

For those of you who are willing to work hard to reach forgiveness, there can be all kinds of benefits. Your relationship with your addicted loved one, and even your relationships with others, should become more peaceful and more positive. In addition, your physical health could improve; recent research shows that forgiveness lowers the forgiver's blood pressure and pulse rate and increases his immune response.

As with other parts of your journey, forgiveness will not be easy. It takes daily practice. Also, the more hurt and pain you have felt, the more threatening it will feel to forgive. You can counteract this fear by reminding yourself that your loving (but healthy) boundaries keep you safe, not your resentments. Forgiveness may leave you vulnerable, but it is the only space from which you can experience true joy.

[Begin exercise 9.1]

Exercise 9.1: Forgiving Your Addicted Loved One

Exercise 8.3 and this exercise concern the same list of behaviors and consequences. In exercise 8.3, you indicated the behaviors and consequences for which you harbor resentments against your addicted loved one. In this exercise, check the boxes next to the behaviors and consequences that you indicated in Exercise 8.3 for which you are willing to forgive your addicted loved one.

Purpose: To assess which feelings of resentment against your addicted loved one you are willing to forgive.

I am willing to forgive my addicted loved one for:

- ❑ Lying to me
- ❑ Manipulating me
- ❑ Stealing from me or others
- ❑ Placating me
- ❑ Bullying me
- ❑ Violating my boundaries
- ❑ Verbally abusing me
- ❑ Destroying property
- ❑ Racking up hospital bills
- ❑ Putting me in the position of having to pay treatment expenses
- ❑ Constantly seeking something from me
- ❑ Displaying poor judgment
- ❑ Embarrassing me
- ❑ Expressing repulsive ideology
- ❑ Flunking out of college
- ❑ Wasting money
- ❑ Taking advantage of my connections in the work world
- ❑ Selling drugs or engaging in other criminal behavior

- ❑ Hurting others I love
- ❑ Treating me and others disrespectfully
- ❑ Destroying my peace of mind
- ❑ Damaging my relationships with others

[End exercise 9.1]

[Begin exercise 9.2]

Exercise 9.2: Forgiving Yourself
Check the boxes next to your behaviors that you are willing to forgive.

Purpose: To assess your behaviors for which you may feel guilty but for which you are willing to forgive yourself.

I am willing to forgive *myself* for:

- ❑ Being in denial
- ❑ Protecting addiction through my actions
- ❑ Blaming my addicted loved one
- ❑ Judging my addicted loved one
- ❑ Ignoring my addicted loved one's trauma
- ❑ Using drugs and/or drinking alcohol with my addicted loved one
- ❑ Trying to control my addicted loved one
- ❑ Tolerating her dishonesty
- ❑ Allowing myself to be manipulated
- ❑ Allowing myself to be badgered and bullied
- ❑ Taking on my addicted loved one's responsibilities
- ❑ Saving my addicted loved one from the consequences of his behavior
- ❑ Buying him things to make him happy
- ❑ Manipulating my addicted loved one
- ❑ Avoiding problems in the name of peace
- ❑ Taking on my addicted loved one's struggle as my own
- ❑ Depriving my addicted loved one of his gift of desperation
- ❑ Making excuses for my addicted loved one's dysfunction
- ❑ Numbing myself instead of looking at the truth
- ❑ Encouraging dependence by my addicted loved one upon me
- ❑ Allowing my fear to control my behavior
- ❑ Failing to respect my addicted loved one's boundaries

- [ ] Being verbally or physically abusive to my addicted loved one
- [ ] Trying to use guilt to manipulate my addicted loved one

[End exercise 9.2]

[Begin exercise 9.3]

Exercise 9.3: Forgiving Others

Complete each of the following sentences that applies with the name of the appropriate person.

Purpose: To help you realize that there are people to whom you have directed resentments for various actions and to state your willingness to forgive them.

I am willing to forgive _____ for introducing my addicted loved one to drugs. I now realize he would have found what he was seeking anyway.

I am willing to forgive _____ for depriving my addicted loved one of the consequences of her behavior.

I am willing to forgive _____ for remaining in denial and delaying the recovery process.

I am willing to forgive _____ for judging my addicted loved one.

I am willing to forgive _____ for rejecting my addicted loved one.

I am willing to forgive _____ for using drugs with my addicted loved one.

I am willing to forgive _____ for causing my addicted loved one pain.

I am willing to forgive _____ for interfering with my attempts to get my addicted loved one help.

I am willing to forgive _____ for engaging in criminal behavior with my addicted loved one.

I am willing to forgive _____ for _____
_____.

[End exercise 9.3]

Chapter 10   Self-care

Self-reflection is stressful.   Making changes in your behavior is exhausting. You can easily lose sight of who you are underneath and what you need during this period of crisis. Thus, self-care is critical for you as well as for your addicted loved one.

Catherine Dotolo, LICSW, an addictions therapist and Clinical Director of Beacon Addictions Advocacy in West Bridgewater, MA, challenges her clients "to look at recovery as encompassing 'self-care,' which ultimately leads all other [family] members to focus on their healing as well."

Likewise, Bruce Dechert, LADC, ICADC, Family Wellness Senior Clinician at Mountainside in Canaan, CT, emphasizes self-care to the family members he sees:

> There are many challenges as we move forward and in this work we need to practice relentless self-focus in order to find the path of recovery. If we falter, if we slip, if we go back to living our lives in fear, we need to reach out, ask for help, and really focus back on ourselves. With recovery, there can be trust, serenity, and hope for those who practice self-care.

Your addicted loved one will thank you later for taking care of yourself. In addition, your self-care may encourage your addicted loved one to seek treatment.   Interventionist Woody Giessmann has found that an addicted individual is "more likely to enter treatment knowing the family is on a journey of health and recovery themselves."

So, pace yourself and keep the larger goal in mind: healing for the whole family. Try to be tolerant with yourself and other family members. Try to remember that you are human and that there is no way to do this perfectly. And, hard as it is, be kind to yourself.

111

In addition to being kind to yourself, self-care includes being patient with yourself, especially during those moments when the whole drama seems so futile—when you simply feel numb or can't seem to stop crying. Those periods are not accidents. This is grieving, and you have plenty to grieve: dashed hopes, lost dreams, and abandoned expectations. Grieving helps you convert painful losses to worthwhile memories.

During times of grieving, it is important to reach out to others for support. The more support the better.

Support groups like Al-Anon and Nar-Anon, the Twelve Step fellowships for family members, as well as Co-Dependents Anonymous and Families Anonymous are available in many communities, and there are online versions of these groups. .Local treatment centers also usually offer support services for families, and even some private clinicians offer group support. All are invaluable.

Members of any of these support groups understand how hard this journey can be at times. These are the people with whom you can be honest. These are the people who can celebrate small triumphs with you and who will understand the despair of setbacks. I encourage you to attend several meetings before selecting a group that feels comfortable or, at least, sort of comfortable.

Finally, friends and family members can also be a great source of support. However, you may need to start the conversation.

[Begin exercise 10.1]

Exercise 10.1: Planning for the Tough Times

Check the boxes next to the support avenue(s) you will choose when you need support.

Purpose: To provide a structure for when your journey is stressful or painful.

When I need to, I will seek the support of a:

- ❑ Therapist or other mental health professional
- ❑ Al-Anon Family Group
- ❑ Member of the clergy
- ❑ Families Anonymous group
- ❑ Nar-Anon Family Group
- ❑ Co-Dependents Anonymous group
- ❑ Community parent action group
- ❑ Treatment center support group
- ❑ Therapeutic support group
- ❑ Church or secular support group
- ❑ Family member
- ❑ Friend

[End exercise 10.1]

Chapter 11   Purpose and Meaning

Many people acknowledge their willingness to endure pain, to surrender, and to forgive when they are able to ascribe a larger meaning to their struggle. Perhaps, like others, you will find that struggle and pain take on different dimensions when you engage in a spiritual practice or serve others.

Religion, spirituality, and philosophy can provide meaning for events that otherwise seem senseless and also can provide a larger meaning to and for your life. Service to others can provide meaning to your life in a different respect: service to others can supply purpose.

When we help others, we feel better about our lives and our experiences. One father realized he was unable to "help" his addicted son without diminishing his son's emerging adulthood. So instead of being fearfully idle, he volunteers his talents to others in recovery. He gives to others what he can't give to his son. It gives him hope for his son and also assigns meaning to his pain.

Similarly, those active in Al-Anon and Nar-Anon often describe their experiences as receiving comfort when they need it and as giving comfort when they have the emotional resources. "Sometimes I go because things are going well with Tessa; other times I go because I need the help," said my friend Dennis.

When we are surrounded by others heading in the same direction, we tend not to feel so alone, desperate, and sorry for ourselves. We gain the understanding that our experiences are not unique, that life is full of suffering, and that, sometimes, all we can do is be open to change. Those who have walked this part of the journey report that they have become better people as a result: more empathetic, compassionate and generous.

Case Study: Mary

Mary first discovered her son's addiction to opiates when he was a teenager. Unsure of what course of action to take, she sought help from any source possible, including books and doctors, psychologists, and other specialists. She realized that her learning curve was behind her son's; each time she thought she had a handle on his problem, he escalated his behavior. Thus, nothing seemed to improve.

Mary talked to other parents but realized they were just as ignorant as she was. So Mary started a community action organization, Parents 4 A Change, in Southington, CT. The organization hosts monthly support group meetings designed to educate parents about opiate addiction and treatment options, and 60-80 people attend each meeting.

As a result of Mary's taking action, many parents in her community have been helped, and she has found her purpose. Often exhausted, Mary continues to be a source of comfort and education for others who find themselves in that particular hell of dealing with a family member's opiate addiction. She comments that she is a better person for her efforts and has found a direction for her life.

Although this isn't the path Mary would have chosen, she keeps sane and productive when her hands and mind are busy. And she has come to believe that "there's always a bigger picture to life than what we may understand at the time."

Chapter 12   The Gifts of Your Journey and Gratitude

I can almost imagine your eyes roll when I talk about the gifts of your journey. Sure, you can see that addiction recovery would be a blessing for your addicted loved one. At a minimum, it would keep him alive. Upon reflection, though, even the most cynical among you should be able to admit there are gifts for you as a result of your journey from denial, fear, protecting, and codependency, even if your addicted loved one never seeks recovery. These gifts can include growth as a person, an appreciation for each moment, deeper relationships with others and yourself, and spirituality.

If you have broken out of denial, surrendered your fear, and forgiven yourself and others, you have grown. You have become less judgmental. You can no longer avoid looking at an addict you pass on the sidewalk. You now know that he is somebody's child, sibling, parent or spouse and probably a wonderful person underneath. When you stopped judging others, you began to appreciate their very real attributes. You became a better person.

Your loved one's addiction has also taught you to live in the moment. If your thoughts keep taking you to the future, your fears of what can happen can grab you by the throat. But if you stay in today, you stay with the thought that your loved one is alive and that, while she is alive, there is always hope. With that thought, you can breathe easily again.

When you stay in the here and right now, you might even look around and find the beauty of today. You might take a moment to soak up the warmth of the sun or to listen to the soothing sound the rain makes as it hits the roof. And you might just have the realization that everything passes. In these moments of inner peace, you know that your life matters as much as your addicted loved one's does.

116

As your journey has progressed, your relationships with others have become more real, more connected, and even more intimate. During your initiation to the world of addiction, you may have tried to hide from others. You stopped hiding when you just couldn't continue to conceal your pain. You have let others in, and you have found that they have stayed even after things smoothed out. You may have reached out to a stranger in need only to find a deep friendship has evolved.

Likewise, your relationship with yourself has deepened. You have learned that you are made of strong stuff. You have weathered a storm you never thought you would have to confront, and you are still standing. Your health may be a little worse, your ego battered, but you are standing. And, standing, you know you can handle the next hardship life throws your way.

Finally, if you have found a deeper spiritual meaning in life, a deeper spiritual connection to a higher power or even a deeper curiosity about a spiritual life, you have received the largest gift of all. With your life expanded enough to allow in the realm of the spiritual, you have opened up a whole other world to explore.

[Begin exercise 12.1]

Exercise 12.1: Gifts of Your Journey
Check the boxes next to the gifts you have received through your journey.

Purpose: To take a moment to reflect on how far you have come.

I have received the following gifts:

- ❑ Teaching me empathy and compassion for others
- ❑ Renewing my relationship with a Higher Power
- ❑ Forcing me to look at my behavior
- ❑ Clarifying my priorities
- ❑ Teaching me how to love another without controlling him
- ❑ Providing my life with a new purpose
- ❑ Teaching me about love
- ❑ Helping me see my addicted loved one for who he is and not just what I wish he would be
- ❑ Making me address my own dysfunctional behavior
- ❑ Encouraging me to appreciate the small things in life
- ❑ Helping me realize that all things are temporary and that all we can do is stay in the moment
- ❑ Encouraging my commitment to staying healthy
- ❑ Teaching me to be accountable for my behavior and to allow others to be accountable for their behavior
- ❑ Teaching me that love is not dependent on someone else's behavior
- ❑ Encouraging me to refocus my attention on myself
- ❑ Teaching me that pain and struggle are unavoidable
- ❑ Teaching me to live life on life's terms
- ❑ Teaching me that my loved one has her own journey as I have mine

[End exercise 12.1]

Case Study: Suzannah

Suzannah, a beautiful, self-possessed woman in her early fifties, came to see me with her husband, Derrick, regarding their middle child Ethan. Growing up, Ethan was a volatile child, and Suzannah described the quality of her days while Ethan was young as being entirely dependent on what kind of a day he was having. Laughing, she explained, "He owned my every mood." When he was calm and well-behaved, she could see the funny, insightful, and often irreverent man he would later become. She also saw in him a wildness and an unwillingness to be accountable for his behavior.

Fast forward two decades. Ethan is in his early twenties, has been to eight treatment centers of various philosophies for various periods of time, and remains an intermittent IV heroin user. Like most addicts with a substantial heroin habit, Ethan engages in disturbing behaviors, including lying, stealing and bullying.

Despite the brutal and lethal experiences Suzannah has been through with Ethan, she possesses a calm grace rarely exhibited by the parents I meet. When asked about it, she explained with an animated intensity, "I have a deep faith in God, and I believe that Ethan will be healed only through his Grace. I finally understand that I cannot be the one to 'fix' him. I am finally ready to let Ethan have his own journey to health and not make it mine. I love him, and I am willing to see him and to feed him when he needs food, but I am unwilling to dedicate my life to the fruitless, impossible task of trying to make him better. I refuse to let this situation steal all joy from this gift of life that I have been given!"

Because Suzannah maintains her faith, she has been able to keep her heart open and her commitment to her relationship with Ethan alive. Her boundaries limit her exposure to the sick sides of Ethan, and her faith ensures that both her heart remains open and her love for him fully alive.

Gratitude

Robert A. Emmons, Ph.D., a leading researcher and writer in the field of gratitude and the editor-in-chief of *The Journal of Positive Psychology*, has found that the regular and deliberate practice of gratitude yields many benefits in the areas of physical health and emotional well-being. One simple way to practice gratitude is to keep a "gratitude journal" in which, at least weekly, you describe, with some detail, five people, events, and/or things for which you are grateful. The profound benefits of gratitude, and a gratitude journal in particular, have been documented in research studies of individuals who were tasked with keeping such a journal. Study participants had strengthened immune systems, lower blood pressure, and better sleep patterns. Also, they attained higher levels of positive emotions, felt happier, more optimistic, and more forgiving, and became more socially engaged.

Simple, however, does not mean easy. When you are in the midst of crisis and trauma it is very difficult to carve out the space necessary for thoughts, feelings and expressions of gratitude. Being grateful and expressing gratitude, however, are worth the effort and will enhance your life long after the crisis has passed. As conveyed by a coaching professional, Sarah Stewart, MSW, CPC, www.coachingwomenthroughchange.com, "To get good at most things you have to practice every day, even when you really don't feel like it. Gratitude is not any different. You have to practice it daily, sometimes more than once, and especially when you don't feel like it."

Final Thoughts

There is no conclusion to this book because the truth is that addiction and recovery have no end. I wish I could promise you that if you would follow a prescribed set of steps your addicted loved one would be well. But I can't. All I can do is urge you to stay on your journey even when it hurts because it is worth it. It is worth it. And when you fall down, and you will fall down, remember it is not by the falling down that we are measured but by the getting back up.

You all are in my thoughts.

Reference Material and Works Cited

Adams, Jane, Ph.D., *When Our Grown Kids Disappoint Us: Letting Go of Their Problems, Loving Them Anyway, and Getting on with Our Lives.* NY: Free Press, 2003

Ashner, Laurie & Meyerson, Mitch, *When Parents Love Too Much: Freeing Parents and Children to Live Their Own Lives.* MN: Hazelden, 1997

Ashner, Laurie & Meyerson, Mitch, *When is Enough Enough?: What You Can Do If You Never Feel Satisfied.* MN: Hazelden, 1996

Baugh, Laura, *Out of the Rough: An Intimate Portrait of Laura Baugh and Her Sobering Journey.* TN: Rutledge Hill Press, 1999

Beattie, Melody, *Codependent No More: How to Stop Controlling Others and Start Caring for Yourself*, 2d Ed. MN: Hazelden, 1992

Beattie, Melody, *The Language of Letting Go: Daily Meditations on Codependency.* MN: Hazelden, 1990

Benton, Sarah Allen, *Understanding the High-Functioning Alcoholic.* CT: Praeger Publishers, 2009

Bill P., Todd W. & Sara S., *Drop The Rock: Removing Character Defects, Steps Six and Seven.* MN: Hazelden, 2005

Black, Claudia, Ph.D., *Family Strategies: Practical Tools for Professionals Treating Families Impacted by Addiction.* CA: Mac Publishing, 2006

Black, Claudia, Ph.D., *It Will Never Happen to Me: Growing Up with Addiction as Youngsters, Adolescents, Adults.* MN: Hazelden, 2001

Bosco, Antoinette, *Radical Forgiveness.* NY: Orbis Books, 2009

Bottke, Allison, *Setting Boundaries with Your Adult Children: Six Steps to Hope and Healing for Struggling Parents.* OR: Harvest House Publishers, 2008

Brown, James, *This River.* CA: Counterpoint, 2010

Caffrey, Patrick, *Beyond Denial: Why Addicts Relapse.* GA: Paraclete Counseling Center Press, 2009

Cermak, Timmen L., *Diagnosing and Treating co-dependence: A Guide for Professionals Who Work with Chemical Dependents, Their Spouses, and Children.* MN: Hazelden, 1998

Cloud, Henry, MD, & Townsend, John, MD, *Boundaries: When to Say Yes, How to Say No to Take Control of Your Life.* MI: Zondervan, 1992

Cohen, Peter R., MD, *Helping Your Chemically Dependent Teenager Recover: A Guide for Parents and Other Concerned Adults.* MN: Hazelden, 1998

Coleman, Bill, *Parents with Broken Hearts: Helping Parents of Prodigals to Cope.* IN: BMH Books, 2007

Conyers, Beverly, *Addict in the Family: Stories of Loss, Hope, and Recovery.* MN: Hazelden, 2003

Conyers, Beverly, *Everything Changes: Help for Families of Newly Recovering Addicts.* MN: Hazelden, 2009

Frankl, Viktor E., *Man's Search for Meaning.* NY: Touchstone, 1984

Frederiksen, Lisa, *If You Loved Me, You'd Stop!: What You Really Need to Know When Your Loved One Drinks Too Much.* CA: KLJ Publishing, 2008

Hansen, Rick, *Buddha's Brain: The Practical Neuroscience of Happiness, Love & Wisdom.* CA: New Harbinger Publications, Inc., 2009

Hanson, Dirk, *The Chemical Carousel: What Science Tells Us About Beating Addiction.* Dirk Hanson, 2008

Jay, Debra, *No More Letting Go: The Spirituality of Taking Action Against Alcoholism and Drug Addiction.* NY: Bantam Dell, 2006

Jay, Jeff & Jay, Debra, *Love First: A Family's Guide to Intervention.* MN: Hazelden, 2000

Johnston, Nancy, MS, *disentangle: When You've Lost Yourself in Someone Else.* NV: Central Recovery Press, 2011

Katherine, Anne, M.A, *Boundaries, Where You End and I Begin: How to Recognize and Set Healthy Boundaries.* NY: Fireside, 1993

Kettelhack, Guy, *First Year Sobriety: When All That Changes is Everything.* MN: Hazelden, 1992

Larsen, Earnie, *Stage II Recovery: Life Beyond Addiction.* NY: HarperCollins Publishers, 1985

Lawford, Christopher Kennedy, *Moments of Clarity: Voices from the Front Lines of Addiction and Recovery.* NY: HarperCollins Publishers, 2009

Linden, David J., *The Compass of Pleasure.* NY: The Penguin Group (USA) Inc., 2011

Mason, Paul, MS & Kreger, Randi, *Stop Walking On Eggshells: Taking Your Life Back When Someone You Care About Has Borderline Personality Disorder.* CA: New Harbinger Publications, Inc., 2010

Maté, Gabor, MD, *In the Realm of Hungry Ghosts: Close Encounters with Addiction.* CA: North Atlantic Books, 2008

May, Gerald, MD, *Addiction & Grace: Love and Spirituality in the Healing of Addictions.* NY: HarperCollins Publishers, 1991

Meyers, Robert J., Ph.D. & Wolfe, Brenda L., Ph.D., *Get Your Loved One Sober: Alternatives to Nagging, Pleading, and Threatening.* MN: Hazelden, 2004

Milam, James R., Ph.D. & Ketcham, Katherine, *Under The Influence: A Guide to the Myths and Realities of Alcoholism.* NY: Bantam Books, 1983

Miller, Angelyn, MA, *The Enabler: when helping hurts the ones you love*, 3d Ed. AZ: Wheatmark, 2008

Moyers, William Cope, *Broken: My Story of Addiction and Redemption.* NY: Penguin Group (USA) Inc., 2006

Nakken, Craig, *Reclaim Your Family From Addiction: How Couples and Families Recover Love and Meaning.* MN: Hazelden, 2000

Newberg, Andrew, M.D. & Waldman, Mark Robert, *How God Changes Your Brain.* NY: Ballantine Books, 2009

O'Neil, Mike & Newbold, Charles E., *Boundary Power: How I Treat You, How I Let You Treat Me, How I Treat Myself.* TN: Sonlight, 1994

Rubin, Charles, *Don't Let Your Kids Kill You*, 3d Ed. CA: NewCentury Publishers, 2008

Sandor, Richard, S., M.D., *Thinking Simply About Addiction.* NY: Penguin Group (USA) Inc., 2009

Schenker, Mark, *A Clinician's Guide to 12-Step Recovery.* NY: W. W. Norton & Company, Inc., 2009

Shapiro, Rami, *Recovery–the sacred art: The Twelve Steps as Spiritual Practice.* VT: Skylight Paths Publishing, 2009

Sheff, David, *beautiful boy: a father's journey through his son's addiction.* NY: Houghton Mifflin Company, 2008

Sheff, David, *clean: Overcoming Addiction and Ending America's Greatest Tragedy.* NY: Houghton Mifflin Harcourt Publishing Company, 2013

Strauch, Barbara, *The Primal Teen: What the New Discoveries about the Teenage Brain Tell Us about Our Kids.* NY: Anchor Books, 2004

Talbot, Jill, *Loaded: Women and Addiction.* CA: Seal Press, 2007

Twerski, Abraham, MD, *Addictive Thinking: Understanding Self-Deception.* MN: Hazelden, 1997

Wegscheider-Cruse, Sharon & Cruse, Joseph, MD, *Understanding Codependency: The Science Behind It and How to Break the Cycle.* FL: Health Communications, Inc., 2012

Weinhold, Barry K., PhD & Weinhold, Janae B., PhD, *Breaking Free of the Co-dependency Trap*, Rev. Ed. CA: New World Library, 2008

White, William L., *Pathways from the Culture of Addiction to the Culture of Recovery: A Travel Guide for Addiction Professionals*, 2d Ed. MN: Hazelden, 1996

Williamson, Marianne, *The Gift Of Change: Spiritual Guidance for Living Your Best Life.* NY: HarperCollins Publishers, 2004

Glossary of Designations Used in this Book

The following gives the generally understood meanings for the designations applied to individuals in this book:

CADC: Certified Alcohol and Drug Counselor

CAP: Certified Addiction Professional

CIP: Certified Intervention Professional

CPC: Certified Professional Coach

ICADC: Internationally Certified Alcohol and Drug Counselor

LADC: Licensed Alcohol and Drug Counselor

LADC-I: Licensed Alcohol and Drug Counselor (highest level)

LCSW: Licensed Clinical Social Worker

LICSW: Licensed Independent Clinical Social Worker

LMHC: Licensed Mental Health Clinician

About the Author

Diana Clark specializes in addiction and families. Diana designed and developed the Family Healing Strategies workshops specifically for family members of addicts and alcoholics, and she facilitates the workshops in conjunction with addiction services facilities/programs across the East Coast. Diana has helped hundreds of families through the Family Healing Strategies workshops, her audio book "What Love Looks Like: When Your Adult Child Struggles with Addiction," her lecture series, and her intervention and individual family coaching services.

Diana is a force of clear speech, logic, and loving acceptance, moving families to engage in behaviors that aid in the recovery process. She offers a calm, compassionate and logical voice during a time of family turmoil.

With a Master's Degree in Counseling Psychology from Antioch University New England Graduate School, Diana has experience as a therapist, interventionist, and consultant addressing issues of addiction and chemical dependency. Prior to her work in counseling psychology, she was a practicing labor and employment attorney, advising employers about the need for well-defined, compassionate, and enforceable workplace policies.

Made in the USA
Columbia, SC
01 April 2018